# NEIGHBOURS

# NEIGHBOURS

Four lectures delivered by
CONOR CRUISE O'BRIEN
in memory of
Christopher Ewart-Biggs

*Introduction by* Jane Ewart-Biggs

*Edited by* Thomas Pakenham

FABER AND FABER
London and Boston

*First published in 1980*
*by Faber and Faber Limited*
*3 Queen Square London WC1N 3AU*
*Printed in Great Britain by*
*Willmer Brothers Limited, Rock Ferry, Merseyside*
*All rights reserved*

*British Library Cataloguing in Publication Data*

O'Brien, Conor Cruise
Neighbours.
1. Great Britain—Foreign relations—Ireland
2. Ireland—Foreign relations—Great Britain
I. Title    II. Pakenham, Thomas
327.41'0417        DA47.9.175

ISBN 0–571–11645–0

# CONTENTS

# INTRODUCTION

*by Jane Ewart-Biggs*

The lectures which make up this book were the gift of one man to the memory of another. Conor Cruise O'Brien wrote and delivered them as his own contribution to the memorial set up for my husband, Christopher, killed by a land mine placed under his car soon after taking up his appointment as British Ambassador to Ireland in 1976.

Christopher was a writer and a diplomat—perhaps in that order. Words were an important ingredient in his life. Choosing them caused him infinite concern. Choosing words which would best convey a true picture of events in his dispatches and telegrams to the Foreign Office. Words which would best convey the humour which formed such an intrinsic part of his personality.

Before becoming Ambassador in Dublin he had served in various posts in the Middle East, North Africa and Europe. He wrote novels when he had time and kept a journal—painstakingly typed by himself at weekends. This journal recounted how a diplomat carries out his day-to-day business. Some of the places in which he served provided backgrounds to his novels. (He spent some years at the outset of his diplomatic career in the

9

# Introduction

Persian Gulf and the novel which he subsequently wrote
fell foul of the Irish censor on the grounds of a beach
scene being described in an over-colourful style. He was
both amused by this and gratified at having at least something in common with certain of the great Irish writers.)
Christopher seemed the prototype of the British diplomat; almost a caricature—tall, angular, with a black
monocle covering the loss of his right eye as a result of a
war-wound. But this conservative coating contained a
radical inside. He hinted something of this when chat-
ting to press correspondents the day before he was
killed: 'British diplomats are in some mysterious way
not supposed to have political views. But I suppose they
are allowed some personal ideas. Mine are liberal with a
small "l". My political philosophy belongs somewhere on
the centre left.' And of his most fundamental sensitivity
—his attitude towards violence—he said, 'things I saw
in Algeria and in the war have given me one strong
prejudice—a prejudice against violence.'

In his profession he combined a total dedication to his
work with a political astuteness and the sense of humour
for which he was so much loved. Lord Greenhill, former
Permanent Under Secretary to the Foreign Office, in his
Memorial address at St Margaret's, Westminster, said:
'He was above all a man of great seriousness of purpose.
He never lost sight of the serious objective, but the way
to it was illuminated by laughter and not dimmed by
tears.'

We did not expect the appointment to Dublin. His
early career in the Foreign Office as an Arabist had
pointed his way to the East and the Arab world. He explained his own reaction in his journal: 'It is Dublin. It

sounds interesting at least; possibly dangerous. Something I could, I think, do. One can at least perform in the best medium, English. There will be a lot to learn though, I have never followed the Irish affair. My resolution will be to avoid agitation, internal and external.' He confided to friends his sense of satisfaction and joy at being given the opportunity of contributing directly, through his profession, towards peace.

When he arrived, he told press correspondents, 'I see my role here as an exercise in clarification. I do not believe in the diplomacy of evasion. I very much do not believe in diplomats being cut off from the life of the country in which they live. I realize that, despite all the common features and the friendliness with which I have been met here, I am in a country which in a paradoxical way may be harder than most for an Englishman to understand.'

What he wrote in his journal for those fifteen days in Dublin seemed to demonstrate an urgency—a compulsion to get down to work and achieve as much as possible. On 9 July he presented his credentials to President O'Dálaigh. 'I say to the President that I will do all that I can, all the time, to try to ensure that our two countries whose interests are so closely interwoven shall always have the comfort of truth and trust together; that we shall know each other's minds as true friends do and that our relationship will be directed to our common future as partners in Europe.' 11 July. He describes his early meetings and discussions with Dr Garret FitzGerald, the Minister for Foreign Affairs, concerning European policies and concerning Northern Ireland. 'All this produces material for two telegrams. So I have started swimming at once.' 12 July. A meeting with officers of the Garda to find out how they estimated his security risk. 'They are not very reassuring. They do not seem to have given much thought to the scenario of attack. They thought for some reason that an attack on the car was unlikely ("It hasn't happened yet"). It seems to be the department of fingers crossed.'

On 21 July, he was killed.

I felt an overwhelming need to build something in the void left by Christopher's death; in some small way to balance the utter negativity of his destruction with something positive and creative. His work would have been for Ireland. Then what we built must be for Ireland. On 29 July many Irish Ministers came to the Residence, at my invitation, following the great service in St Patrick's Cathedral: Dr Garret FitzGerald, Mr Jack Lynch, Dr Conor Cruise O'Brien were among them. Thomas Pakenham, whose inspiration it was, asked them there and then for their support for a Memorial Fund in Christopher's name whose objects would be to promote the ideals to which he dedicated himself: peace and understanding in Ireland; stronger links between the peoples of Britain and Ireland; and closer co-operation between the partners of the European Community. The Fund would be used to finance an annual prize to be awarded to the writer whose recent work would be considered by a panel of judges to contribute most to promote these ideals. The Memorial was thus made to fit the man whom it honoured.

The Memorial was launched, sponsored and subscribed to by leading Irishmen. Proof of how the ordinary people of Ireland felt about it came through the postman. I received nearly a thousand letters from Ireland. Envelopes containing postal orders, single pound notes—even coins—accompanied by letters offering me the sorrow of Ireland. 'You may be weeping your lost husband,' one said, 'but we are weeping our lost honour.' Others demonstrated the wish of Irish people to respond to the spirit of peace and reconciliation represented by the Memorial. '. . . and we shall all, individually and collectively, continue in our work for Truth and Peace with renewed purpose.' And, 'It is for the Irish people now to try and follow up his ideals.' For, after all, it was a Memorial designed not simply to commemorate a name but more to reflect the tolerance and moderation for which Christopher had stood and out of which a state of reconciliation and peace is born.

After we had established the Memorial Trust in Ireland we extended it to London, Paris and Brussels. We received hundreds more letters of sympathy and support. It seemed right that this prize about peace and understanding in Ireland should benefit from the wider European dimension. Christopher had believed the new European relationship between Britain and Ireland would form the basis for his work in Dublin. He saw how the shared hopes and mutual interests were binding the two countries closer together and believed this new partnership would help in the work to be done to bring peace to Northern Ireland.

In response to our appeal, we received a total of £39,000. Officially recognized as a charity, the Trust was soon in a position to offer an annual prize of £1,500, and we gave the administration of this prize to the National Book League. We established an international panel of judges: Graham Greene, Seamus Heaney, Máire Cruise O'Brien, Thomas Pakenham, Maurice Schumann of the

## *Introduction*

French Academy and Georges Sion of the Royal Academy of Literature in Brussels. I am most grateful to all of them—not only for their hard work but also for all the kindness they have shown me since the conception of this Memorial Prize.

The Memorial is now in its fourth year, and has so far been won each year by Irish writers. In 1977 the prize was shared by Father Michael MacGréil for his *Prejudice and Tolerance in Ireland* and A. T. Q. Stewart for *The Narrow Ground.* In 1978 the winner was Dervla Murphy nominated for her *A Place Apart.* Merlyn Rees presented the prize at Chatham House in London. In 1979 the prize went to Stewart Parker for his television play *I'm a Dreamer Montreal.* The prize was presented at Trinity College, Dublin, by Mr Jack Lynch, then Taoiseach.

I hope that each of these works has helped to create better understanding between peoples and that in future years writers of every kind—authors, playwrights, journalists, etc.—will continue to send us their work. We feel that the need for this Memorial Prize has not diminished. In the words of Mr Jack Lynch, presenting the 1979 prize, 'Everything that we can do to replace mistrust with reconciliation, hatred with tolerance, alienation with affection will contribute to preventing the divisions, which have caused such suffering, from being passed on to further generations.'

The four Memorial Lectures contained in this book have added another dimension to our Memorial.

Conor Cruise O'Brien never met Christopher. During those tragically short weeks in Dublin, Christopher did not have time to meet the author of the books which he had read with so much admiration. Had they known each other, their friendship would have been assured. I can think of no man more fitted to pay tribute to his memory. All of us—the Trustees of the Memorial and myself—owe him our deepest gratitude for having made us the present of these lectures, so masterly an expression of his own courageous views.

The lectures were delivered from four points of vantage : Dublin in January 1978, Belfast in June 1978, New York in November 1978 and Oxford in October 1979. I shall not try to summarize the far-ranging contents. But let me support the conclusions; views which were Christopher's too. There can never be a justification for political violence. It is not only evil but self-defeating. And it can but be destructive to us all, Catholics, Protestants, Irish and British. This Memorial is dedicated not only to Christopher but to all those others who have died violently in the last ten years, both the well-known public men and the ordinary people whose lives have been sacrificed and whose families have been left to mourn.

In conclusion I would like to thank those many people who have all in some way or other helped me with this Memorial. I would like to thank them not only for their practical help but also for all the interest, encouragement and kindness they have shown me. I have kept my final thanks for Thomas Pakenham whose inspiration it was to build this Memorial; and, in so doing, contrived not only to create a fitting tribute to a good and highly civilized man, but also to put something real into my own life.

# 1

## The Outlook from West to East:
## One Aspect of Irish-British Relations

*Delivered at Trinity College, Dublin,*
*17 January 1978*

This is the first of a series of four lectures which I shall be giving in memory of Christopher Ewart-Biggs. The lectures will deal with various aspects of British-Irish relations. This first lecture will principally concern itself with attitudes in the Republic of Ireland towards Britain and the British. The second lecture, in Belfast, will deal with the special problem of Northern Ireland, within the general context of British-Irish relations. The third lecture, in New York, will be concerned with the question of Ireland in the wider context of British-American and Irish-American relations. The fourth and final lecture, in Oxford, will deal with British attitudes towards Ireland, both North and South.

These lectures are commemorative in a double sense. First they commemorate a notably gifted and notably attractive human being, cut off, to all our loss, just as he was entering on a momentous task, in which there is every reason to believe that he, his gifts and his personality would have made a very significant contribution to the improvement of relations between the two countries. I did not myself know Christopher Ewart-Biggs, but since very shortly after his death, my wife and I have felt that we have in some spiritual sense come to know him, through our friendship with his gallant and magnanimous widow, Jane.

The second aspect of the commemoration is more impersonal, but it is an aspect which Christopher Ewart-Biggs, as a dedicated diplomat, would have wished us to consider. We are commemorating, as well as a human being, also an *event*—a peculiarly ominous and symbolic event: the murder of an envoy.

In all ages and in all cultures, I believe the murder of an envoy has been regarded as a peculiarly heinous crime, graver in its implications even than other categories of murder. It violates immemorial laws of hospitality, vital to our tenuous and threatened sense of human solidarity. It endangers other human lives. It damages, in a great number of ways, relations between states, between communities, between people. But it is also symptomatic. It registers the existence of a pathological element in the relations between two peoples.

In examining certain Irish attitudes towards Britain, I shall have in mind the existence of that pathological element, and seek to identify and describe it.

It was an Irish vision of England that killed Christopher Ewart-Biggs. He died not because of what he was, but because of how the country which he represented could be seen in the country in which he represented it. Some of you may well feel uneasy with that formulation. The murder of the Ambassador was the act of a tiny band of hardened fanatics, and was regarded with horror by the great majority of Irish people.

That is quite true. None the less, it was an Irish vision of England that killed Christopher Ewart-Biggs, and that

17

vision is by no means confined to the fanatical conspirators who were the instruments of the deed. The conspirators are possessed by that vision in an intense form. Many of the rest of us are pervaded by a nebulous form of it.

The possessed draw their strength from the pervaded.

The possessed derive, from the intensity of the vision which grips them, an abundant sense of justification. Since England is synonymous with guilt and oppression, any blow against England, however terrible it may seem, is a blow for righteousness and liberty.

The pervaded flinch from the horrors perpetrated, but feed the sense of justification that makes it possible to go on perpetrating them. They agree that England is responsible for the unjust partition of this country, which is presented as the cause of all the violence. They agree that it was the gun which won us the freedom we have in this part of the country.

When the possessed ask the pervaded why the same methods which, as they both agree, won us this part of the country should not be used now to win back from England the unjustly partitioned part, the pervaded— by reason of their pervasion—can have no honest or effective answer. Their inability to answer fortifies the possessed not only in their sense of justification, but also in their pride of being an elite who act on assumptions which other Irishmen claim to share but have not the courage to act on. So fortified, the possessed keep up the killing. The pervaded reprove them for this periodically, but pay tribute to their idealism. So well they might.

The rhetoric of the pervaded is the dominant rhetoric here, both in politics and in the media. How far does pervasion extend among the public generally? In other words, how widely are anti-English attitudes prevalent among us?

Now here, I shall have to draw on a source on which I have also drawn—at the recent British-Irish Association conference—at Oxford. The reason why I have to draw on it again is simple. The information about the attitudes of Dubliners contained in Father MacGréil's *Prejudice and Tolerance in Ireland* constitutes the only solid and reasonably detailed body of information available about the range of attitudes of any Irish people on such matters as those with which I am concerned in this lecture.

Father MacGréil's survey was carried out in Dublin in 1972. At first sight, the results of his survey look most encouraging, from the viewpoint of those who hope for improvement in Anglo-Irish relations. Clearer inspection, however, reveals some ominous features.

At the level of inter-personal relations, the results show extremely favourable attitudes towards the English and the British, in that order. The crucial question in the interview-questionnaire concerned the declared willingness of the respondent to admit a member of a given social group to his or her family. By this criterion, the English are more favoured by Dubliners than is any other 'attitude' group. Of the respondents, 87.3 per cent say they would admit English people to their family. 'British' is the next most acceptable category at 82.4 per cent. The Northern Irish follow at 79.5 per cent, well behind the English and just ahead of the Welsh and Scots, who tie at 78.4 per cent. Of the world outside the archipelago, the French are most favoured (74.1 per cent), followed by Yanks (69.9 per cent). In the light of the 'acceptability' responses, it is not surprising that 89 per cent of respondents regard the British as 'a pretty decent people'.

Those are all declared reactions to propositions about English or British *people*. Reactions to the more abstract concept of 'Britain' and to the British *Government* are more adverse. Of the respondents, 62 per cent disagree and only 30 per cent agree with the proposition that 'the world owes a lot to Britain'. While 54.7 per cent disagree with the proposition : 'I don't object to the British people but I don't like the British Government', 36.2 per cent agree with it and 9.1 per cent don't know. And though 79.3 per cent disagreed with the proffered statement : 'I would be happy if Britain were brought to her knees', 17.1 per cent agreed with that chilling proposition.

In this lecture the group that will concern me most is that 17.1 per cent.

Two of the aggregated answers to these questions bring us, I believe, as near as we can get for the moment to knowing the relative extent of Anglophilia and Anglophobia in this country.[1]

I am disposed, but rather tentatively, to identify the proportion of Anglophiles at 30 per cent—the percentage of those who agreed with the proposition that 'the world owes a lot to Britain'. If you take the answer at its face-value, it is the answer, not merely of an Anglophile, but of an Anglophile's Anglophile. I am myself judged by some of our fellow countrymen to be sorely deficient in Anglophobia, but I must admit I would have hesitated long before answering that question. Granted that

[1] The MacGréil survey is of Dubliners, but as so many Dubliners are of recent and varied rural origin, it can be taken—in the absence of a corresponding national survey—as the best guide we have to Irish attitudes on the matter.

Britain's contributions to the world have been enormous, so also the world's contributions to Britain have been enormous, and not always voluntary. Is it the world that is the net debtor, or Britain? How much does Shakespeare weigh against the slave-trade? How much does Britain's leading part in abolishing the slave-trade weigh against Britain's earlier leading part in carrying on the slave-trade? Who is to say, who owes who what—and what is the use of saying it anyway? Lost in such speculations I fear I should eventually have drifted into the 'don't know' lobby. Compared to me, it would appear that 30 per cent of the people of Dublin are positive Blimps. It would appear so, that is, were one to take such an answer altogether literally. Another answer, though in itself perplexing, may none the less help to correct the perspective. Among the respondents, 85 per cent agreed with the proposition : 'I have no particular love or hate of the British'. It would appear from this that if our 30 per cent are Anglophiles, at least half of them do not wish to admit to this proclivity. However, the question about 'no particular love or hate' is inherently confusing and Father MacGréil himself points out that respondents were 'quite confused' by it : he also points out that the answers to it correlate positively with responses affirming that 'the British are a pretty decent people'.

Without, therefore, exaggerating the intensity of Anglophilia in the 30 per cent, one can nevertheless identify this proportion as highly resistant to the traditional Irish Republican anti-British view of history and of the world. In the terms I used at the outset, these are the unpervaded.

The attribute of Anglophobia defines itself more crisply. There can be no doubt about that 17.1 per cent which 'would be happy if Britain were brought to her knees'. I find that figure startlingly and frighteningly high. If I had been asked what proportion of contemporary Dubliners would declare themselves to be 'happy' about that, I should have guessed about 5 or 6 per cent; the actual figure (for 1972) is about three times that. It is true that the sentiment is a traditional one. There is an anonymous Gaelic quatrain, from the seventeenth or eighteenth century, which vividly expresses this particular aspiration. Let me quote it, in my wife's translation:

*May we never taste of death nor leave this vale of tears*
*Until we see the Englishry go begging down the years,*
*Packs on their backs to earn a penny pay*
*In little leaking boots—as the Irish in their day.*

It is the wish of the oppressed against the oppressor, anywhere and at any time. But in the case of 17.1 per cent of Dubliners, the wish has long outlasted the oppression.

That the wish should survive in some kind of vague half-life in the Irish psyche is something easily understood, but in the case of this section it is strong enough to be blurted out. This is significant of intensity. In general, people's answering tends (I believe) to emphasize the 'niceness' or 'respectability' of the respondent. The avowal of a vindictive sentiment like this is therefore a danger signal. These people feel bloodyminded even to the extent that they don't mind showing themselves in that light. This raises the disturbing possibility that, if we allow for a certain number of people who are equally hostile, but more cautious about revealing the fact, the proportion of real Anglophobes is even somewhat higher than that 17.1 per cent. Other responses suggest that this may indeed be so. Some 22.1

per cent of the respondents agreed with the proposition that 'some British qualities are admirable, but on the whole I don't like them' (74.5 per cent, however, disagreed); 20 per cent declared themselves not 'happy to see British people get on in Ireland' (74 per cent were happy); 28 per cent agreed that 'British soldiers are generally cruel and brutal'; 57 per cent disagreed. In this last case, considering that the interviewing was carried out within a year of Bloody Sunday, the majority disagreeing seems more significant than the 28 per cent minority agreeing; and that 28 per cent is, I believe, considerably larger than the proportion of genuine Anglophobes.

Considering the various answers, I would put genuine Anglophobes—the possessed and the heavily pervaded together—at around 20 per cent of the population. I have assessed the unpervaded (or negligibly pervaded) at around 30 per cent.

If these assessments are approximately correct, the remaining half of the population could be described as lightly pervaded: remarkably well-disposed towards English and British people but responsive in varying degrees to invitations to view 'Britain' and 'the British Government' with aversion.

It is true of course that some respondents show themselves apparently 'Anglophile' on some points and 'Anglophobe' on others. This 11.1 per cent think the British are a pretty decent people, but on the whole don't like them; 6.1 per cent think they are pretty decent, but would be happy to see Britain brought to its knees; 9.4 per cent would admit British people to their families, but on the whole don't like them; 4.4 per cent would admit British

23

people to their families, but would be happy to see Britain brought to its knees. . . .

The apparent contradictions in the responses about British people and Britain are ascribed by Father Mac-Gréil to what he calls 'post-colonial attitudinal schizophrenia'. I cannot altogether accept that formula, for reasons I shall come to. But it is certain there can be, in an Irish mind, strong tensions between pro-British and anti-British attitudes.

Forty years ago the poet Yeats described these tensions in the following words :

> No people hate as we do in whom that past is always alive, there are moments when hatred poisons my life and I accuse myself of effeminacy because I have not given it adequate expression. It is not enough to have put it into the mouth of a rambling peasant poet. Then I remind myself that though mine is the first English marriage I know of in the direct line, all my family names are English, and that I owe my soul to Shakespeare, to Spenser and to Blake, perhaps to William Morris, and to the English language in which I think, speak, and write, that everything I love has come to me through English; my hatred tortures me with love, my love with hate. I am like the Tibetan monk who dreams at his initiation that he is eaten by a wild beast and learns on waking that he himself is eater and eaten.

I don't know how the poet would have reacted if someone had told him he was suffering from a simple case of 'post-colonial attitudinal schizophrenia'.

Yeats's ascendance, as he himself reminds us, was that of *colon* as distinct from *colonisé*, in Fanon's terminology, but many of the English-speaking descendants of the *colonisés* would have to recognize similar symptoms in themselves. Yet labels based on the concept of 'colonialism' can be of only limited assistance, because of the enormous varieties of human experience covered by that general term. The heir to the Ashanti kingdom was four years old when British troops first entered his capital of Kumasi; he lived to be Asantehene, chief of his people, in what is now the second city of the Republic of Ghana. He personally had seen the British come, and he had seen them go. It was a colonial experience certainly, but very different from the Irish one. Nor would most Irish people see it as anything *but* very different. There is a rhetoric according to which Irish people readily identify with the peoples of Asia and Africa, because of our common experience of the evils of British imperialism. There is a certain limited amount of truth in this, for some Irish people, but Father MacGréil's survey appears to show that most Dubliners, at least, prefer, personally speaking, to identify themselves with the imperialist rather than with the fellow victims of imperialism. You will remember that the percentage of respondents declaring themselves willing to accept English people into their families was 87.3—the highest recorded in the survey. The comparable figures for the other identifiable peoples of the former Empire covered in the survey (omitting only 'Yanks') are as follows:

| | |
|---|---|
| Indians | 28.5% |
| Pakistanis | 23.9% |
| Zambians | 23.1% |
| Nigerians | 22.4% |

The tendency to identify with the rulers rather than the ruled is not altogether paradoxical. Irish people had been among the rulers. They made—as their spokesmen

once used to boast—a notable contribution to the building of the British Empire. Many of them died for it.
Among the heirlooms of the Asantehene was the severed
head of Sir Charles McCarthy, commander of the British
forces in the First Ashanti War. Some made others die.
The most execrated figure in the eyes of Indian nationalists in the twentieth century was General O'Dwyer, who
gave the order that brought about the massacre at
Amritsar. Of course, in the Irish Republican perspective,
these were renegades, bad Irishmen. Republicans would
be unwise to insist too much upon that, since the Father
of Irish Republicanism did his best to be of the number
of those renegades, through his project for a British mili-
tary colony in the South Seas. If that project had not
been ignored by Pitt, Theobald Wolfe Tone would have
been among the minor pillars of the Empire. Roger Case-
ment was such a pillar, up to his retirement from the
Consular Service.

Participation in the imperial enterprise was not confined to any one community or class. Catholics as well as
Protestants played their part at many different levels, in
the British Army and Navy, in the police, and perhaps
most notably in the mission field. In the days when the
word 'empire' was of good repute, Irish journalists—
especially Catholic and nationalist ones—liked to boast
of Ireland's 'spiritual empire', implicitly or explicitly
contrasted with the coarsely material empire of Ireland's
neighbour. But the confines of the spiritual empire in
modern times were essentially identical (though not
chronologically synchronized) with those of the material
one: Irish missionaries followed wherever English ex-
pansion had brought the English language. In Africa and
Asia they were spreading not only their interpretation of

26

the Gospel, but also Western education, in its Anglo-phone form, a crucial, though ambiguous aspect of the imperial task. There is no other people which thinks—and has reason to think—of itself as an ex-colony which has played so large a part in colonizing other lands, and in the management of a great empire.

If we speak of Ireland today as being 'post-colonial', we should recognize that the word has to be used in a double sense : 'post-colonial' in the sense of having undergone colonial domination, and also 'post-colonial' in the sense of having taken part in colonial domination over others, or contributed to colonial enlightenment if you prefer to contemplate that aspect of a complex phenomenon. The 'schizophrenia' is not just a *post-colonial* thing; it was also there during the colonial period, and is an important part of our historical culture and inheritance.

Yeats's 'schizophrenia' was that of an Irish nationalist conscious and proud of his settler origins : proud of the result of something to which he was opposed in principle.

The anti-British element in the psyche of the majority in the Republic is more elemental. There can be few Irish children of Catholic formation, conscious exclusively or mainly of Gaelic ancestry, who have not, during an early exposure to Irish history, thought to themselves, however vaguely, something like this : 'The English tried to kill our religion and they did kill our language.'

That thought has a deep emotional charge. For a time, at least, we—I speak as one who was once just such a child, improbable as that may now appear to some—for a time we feel about 'the English' as about a force hostile to our very identity. It is a time at which we are likely to

27

find hardly anything excessive in the neat antitheses of that old nationalist catechism:

Q. What is the opposite of heaven?
A. Hell.
Q. What is the opposite of Ireland?
A. England.

Most children who feel like that grow up. Father Mac-Gréil's figures confirm that.

Some children who feel like that do not grow up. Father MacGréil's figures also confirm that.

Those who grow up notice that the contemporary English are readily distinguishable from the subjects of Elizabeth, Cromwell and Queen Anne, and even from those of Queen Victoria and King George V. They also learn that the ancestors of not only the Irish, but most other people, including the English poor, had to endure privation and oppression. They learn that the contemporary English do not care what language the Irish speak or what religion they profess. They realize that, if the Irish of the present day do not revive Gaelic, as a spoken and written vernacular, this is not because the English prevent them from doing so, but because they themselves do not in fact want to do so. They also get to know British and English people, and as the survey figures so plainly demonstrate, they like them, more than anybody except their own selves. And finally, they get to know that the material interests of the Irish of today are intertwined with those of Britain, and that what hurts Britain is likely to hurt us.

In this maturing process, the original Anglophobia diminishes and recedes, often remaining faintly present in the subconscious, but generally without much influence over words and actions. But in the case of some people—that 17.1 per cent—the Anglophobia clearly has not succumbed to a maturing intellectual process.

Why should this be?

The MacGréil responses, at least in their published form, can no longer help us here. I can only therefore offer a hypothesis, based on some decades of personal observation of Irish Anglophobes, of their behaviour, their conversation and their writings. It is a hypothesis capable of being tested by scientific observation, although of a somewhat complex kind. I hope that may be attempted in some future survey.

The hypothesis is that the reason why, in the cases of this minority, emotional Anglophobia does not succumb to a maturing process is that in these cases, maturation is not in fact achieved. That is to say that these are unfortunate people who in varying degrees are either intellectually retarded or emotionally disturbed, perhaps sometimes both. In this condition, they latch on to the past sufferings of the Irish people, cast England in the devil role, project the past into the present, interpret contemporary events in the light of the devil-theory, and satisfactorily account to themselves for how bad they feel; it is all England's doing. They also, I think, derive from the extravagance of their Anglophobia, and the knowledge that this is not shared by most of their fellow-citizens, a certain sad *machismo*; others may have bowed down, they are the faithful few.

Not all of that is capable of empirical testing. But the basic hypothesis of non-maturation could be tested, by asking, along with questions designed to ascertain attitudes, also questions designed to test general intelligence

29

and emotional maturity, and correlating the answers to the two sets of questions.

I hope a survey of that kind may be carried out. I am not, however, inviting Father MacGréil to carry it out. He has suffered enough already. That gentle scholar, himself a devoted patriot, but not of the hating kind, has already had to endure the attentions of detachments from the 17.1 per cent. One person, who has attained a melancholy eminence in that sub-culture, launched an enterprise congenial to his admirers. This was the endeavour to expel Father MacGréil from the Gaelic League for having accepted a Ewart-Biggs literary award. In explaining the attractions of this magnanimous undertaking, this cultural purist began one of his statements with the deftly adjusted classical tag :

*Timeo Anglos et dona ferentes*

Mr O'Snodaigh, for it was he, or if not, it was somebody very like him, was here casting himself in the role of Laocoon, bravely hurling his spear at the Trojan Horse of the Ewart-Biggs Literary Award.

Now, to contemplate the implications of that learned analogy is to peer into the very abyss of paranoia. What it implies is that the contemporary English plot the downfall of Ireland, just as the Greeks of old plotted the fall of Troy. Just as the wily Ulysses devised the Trojan Horse, so the crafty Jim Callaghan is supposed to have thought up the Ewart-Biggs Literary Award. . . .

The imagination of outsiders may boggle, but if you live in the world of the 17.1 per cent it all figures, though it would have to be explained rather carefully and slowly to some of the brethren.

It will be claimed that I attribute too much to historical and psychological factors. We need not, it will be said, look to the past for an explanation of Anglophobia : what is happening now in Northern Ireland is a sufficient explanation in itself.

I shall be dealing with the question of Northern Ireland in my second lecture. Here I am primarily concerned with what might be called the Dublin-London connection. In that context, I think it enough to say that it is not Northern Ireland that causes Anglophobia; it is Anglophobia that projects a false picture of events in Northern Ireland. In that picture, the basic facts of the division and balance between the local communities is ignored or distorted, and replaced by the claim that Ireland is kept divided by British force. This is just a special region of the general world of fantasy of the 17.1 per cent. I do not believe that even if the British were to leave Northern Ireland the Anglophobia of this section would be sensibly diminished. The emphasis would simply shift to some other area among those designated by Sinn Fein; British commercial influence, British cultural influence, our joint membership with Britain in the EEC. The ancient enemy would still be around, craftily disguised, for the faithful to seek out, unmask and denounce. They could not, after all, do without him.

It may also be argued that in looking at the particular aspect of Anglo-Irish relations with which we are here concerned, I have made too much of the 17.1 per cent plus and not enough of, for example, the 83 per cent who like British people. But the point about the 17.1 per cent is that that is where the trouble lies. Certainly in the context of these Memorial Lectures, it would be wrong to minimize it. It is, after all, out of the shadows of that world that there emerged the murderers of Christopher Ewart-Biggs. Out of that world too came the writers

31

who, in the aftermath of that murder, sought to condone or mitigate the murder, in the columns of an Irish national newspaper. That world casts a shadow over our media, our politics, our lives generally. Most of the rest of us are a little afraid of these people and not without reason. It is through that fear as well as through confusion and rhetorical habits that the possessed are able to pervade. One can be physically or morally afraid; or politically afraid. The fear of losing that sizeable vote, or the hope of gaining it, exerts a fairly strong pull over politics, and thereby acts as a disturbing and confusing influence in Irish-British relations. No prudent politician would appeal to these people directly, using their own dialect of hate : to do so would be to alarm the majority who neither hate England nor want trouble. But there are ways of reaching them, discreet signals which attract them without alarming others. The trick is to get yourself seen as 'standing up to John Bull'. This can be done even if poor John Bull is doing no more than vaguely wondering why you are standing up. The point is that the audience aimed at *thinks* of John Bull as a cruel menacing figure, and therefore thinks of the politician as brave for talking tough to him. The politician knows he is running no risks at all. Doing the thing discreetly, he scoops in the 17.1 per cent without frightening off the rest. Not much *direct* damage is done to Anglo-Irish relations. The damage done is mainly internal, in increasing confusion, and in appeasing, flattering and tending to perpetuate a sub-culture which is, in every sense, a pathological element in our life.

I think it likely that increasing prosperity and improving education are reducing the importance of that sub-culture. I believe that if a survey were taken now the 'beaten to their knees' element would *probably* be below the 17.1 per cent recorded in 1972. But perhaps not much lower: one should not underestimate the capacity of those infected to transmit the infection to the next generation.

'Break the connection', wrote Wolfe Tone. 'Only connect', wrote E. M. Forster.

Our need today is not to disconnect but to understand connections, refine them, make them appropriate to mutual needs, not burdensome to any of the great groups connected. Constitutional connections can be broken; geographical connections cannot, nor can the commercial and cultural connections which geography has brought about. The sea which we think of as separating the two islands actually joins them. There is no valid moral reason why contemporary Britain and contemporary Ireland should not enjoy full, open, unreserved friendship. Such a friendship fully acknowledged and steadfastly held, could be of immense benefit to all of us, and most especially to all the people of Northern Ireland.

We have some reason to believe that most of the people of Dublin at least would like to see that happen. We can also identify the element which does not want to let that happen. That element thinks of itself as inimical to Britain only: it is however to Ireland that it does most damage, intellectually and emotionally as well as in other ways. Economic and social forces will, we hope, gradually reduce the influence of that element, eventually remove its veto.

But we should also remember this: that element is most formidable not through its own strident and often barely coherent utterances, but through a quiet process of pervasion—through the silences it is able to create, the discretions it can dictate.

There is an unhealthy system of circumspection surrounding the Anglophobes and partly dominated by them. In this series of lectures I mean to break through that system, and encourage others to do the same in their own way, shrinking the zone of pervasion.

In the circumstances of today, and speaking the language we do speak, to love both Ireland and Britain is not to be a divided man. It is to be a whole man.

# 2

## The Northern Connection in Irish-British Relations

*Delivered at Queen's University, Belfast,*
*23 June 1978*

All my Northern auditors, of whatever tinge or section, are, I think, likely to agree with at least one statement in this address: that which I am now about to make:

'I know relatively little about Northern Ireland.'

Some may also agree that all the same I at least have devoted more attention to Northern Ireland than most of the Southern Irish, including most Southern politicians, have done. That attention has been noted in Northern Ireland, not invariably with approval. It has been borne in upon me that I have aroused, in certain sections, what may be called an oecumenism of vindictiveness. Almost eight years ago now, after I had been physically attacked in Derry, while listening—no doubt imprudently—to speakers at an Apprentice Boys' Rally, I received a post-card from Omagh, Co. Tyrone. It read simply: 'I am glad to see the Prods beat you up in Derry. If you come to Omagh, I can promise you a Catholic beating up.'

It may be reasonably asked why, since I admit to knowing relatively little about Northern Ireland, compared at least with its inhabitants, I have none the less chosen to address an audience here in Belfast on that subject. The answer is that Northern Ireland is an important part, but still only a part, of the subject I wish to discuss here this evening. That subject is the Northern connection: Northern Ireland seen in the context of British-Irish relations generally. In that general area I think I can claim to be reasonably well-informed.

It is through Northern Ireland that Great Britain and Ireland are most obviously connected, though they are connected also in many more impalpable but not less important ways. It is certainly in Northern Ireland that those who seek today to carry out Wolfe Tone's injunction: 'to break the connection with England', most vividly perceive that connection; again, these people do not perceive that connection as exclusively Northern. They have made it clear that their *raison d'être* would not disappear with the departure of British troops from the North, any more than it disappeared with the departure of British troops from the South.

It is certainly appropriate to discuss that connection in the context of these lectures, which commemorate Christopher Ewart-Biggs. Christopher Ewart-Biggs was Ambassador in the Republic of Ireland of the United Kingdom of Great Britain and Northern Ireland. He was the symbol, that is to say, not only of the connection between Great Britain and the sovereign State to which he was accredited, but also of the connection between Great Britain and Northern Ireland, as distinct parts of the sovereign State which he represented. And it is because of what he symbolized that he was murdered.

Those who murdered him were those who follow both Wolfe Tone's injunction and Wolfe Tone's commitment to the use of physical force in breaking the connection. Granted that, it has to be granted also that the murderers were acting with a merciless logic in destroying the living symbol of the connections they are pledged to break by force.

You will understand that in saying that, I am in no way condoning or mitigating that terrible deed. Logic that rests on crazy premises leads to conclusions that are not merely merciless but crazy as well. That I believe to be the case with this particular logic. The need to demonstrate that this is so is one reason—a grimly relevant one in the context of these lectures, but still only one reason —for wishing to consider the nature of the connection, and in this case especially the Northern connection.

I shall indicate some of the other reasons later. For the moment I should like to give some idea of the complexity of the phenomenon to which I refer here as the Northern connection. I am not referring to the constitutional connection, the nature of which is readily understood, whether it is rejected or upheld. What I wish to consider, rather, is the social and political connection, which is made up of multiple entities, relations and attitudes. There are four clearly discernible entities: the people of Great Britain, the people of the Republic, the Protestants of Northern Ireland, the Catholics of Northern Ireland. (I leave the Southern Protestants out of account here because they are as a group no longer clearly distinguishable, in terms of political attitudes and loyalties, from the rest of the population in the Republic.) Mathematically, there are six possible dual inter-relationships among the four entities. In this case the inter-relationships involved are those between Northern Catholics and the Republic, Northern Catholics and Northern Protestants, Northern Catholics and Britain, Northern Protestants and the Republic, Northern Protestants and Britain and finally the

# The Northern Connection

Republic and Britain. As each of these pairs involves two sets of attitudes, there are already twelve sets of attitudes involved. I need not trouble you by enumerating these: they are readily identifiable, if not so readily understandable. But even there, at twelve, the discrimination of relevant sets of attitudes does not cease by any means. There are triangles as well as dualities. For example, it is obviously not possible to understand the attitudes of Northern Catholics towards Britain without taking into account the attitudes of Northern Catholics to Northern Protestants, and also of Northern Protestants to Northern Catholics; nor is it possible to understand that last set of attitudes without understanding the attitudes of Northern Protestants towards the Republic and vice versa. There are also, as well as the complexities, influential simplifications at work: for example, many British people simply do not distinguish either between Catholics and Protestants in Northern Ireland, or indeed between the inhabitants of Northern Ireland and those of the Republic. They lump all the Irish together, often under some more or less opprobrious designation. For them Ireland is indeed that mystical entity once hailed in the title of an anti-partitionist treatise: *The Indivisible Island.* And some of them are quite as willing to break the connection between that other island and their own as any Irish Republican could be.

None the less that connection is not so easily broken. The point I have been trying to hammer home is that the connection is not just a simple bilateral constitutional one—of which the breaking might be thought of as a relatively simple matter—but one involving a complex of historically-informed social entities, relations and attitudes, something not easily to be broken or quickly altered.

Having registered the existence of such complexities, I do not propose to attempt a deeper plunge into them. Instead, I shall, in the main, confine myself to the rather simple concept of the triangle of Great Britain–Northern Ireland–Republic of Ireland—bearing in mind, however, that the triangle, at its apex in Northern Ireland, is liable to turn into a rectangle.

Let me turn first to attitudes in Britain towards Northern Ireland. I have already said something about the general attitudes of the man in the street. The polls confirm that most British people would like to be rid of Northern Ireland. But the issue is still not likely to be determined by opinions articulated in *polls*. It will be determined, as it is determined now, by political forces, gauged by political men. It is true that the 'get rid of Northern Ireland' opinion of the British public in general could become such a force if the people holding the opinion held it with sufficient intensity. But they do not so hold it. Just as in the Republic the aspiration to acquire Northern Ireland is a low-intensity aspiration, so in Great Britain the aspiration to get rid of Northern Ireland is a low-intensity aspiration. Both have, therefore, low priorities in terms of practical politics. The Provisional IRA thought they could give the question a higher priority, thus giving impetus to withdrawal, by a bombing campaign in mainland Britain. As might be expected, they badly miscalculated the psychology of British people. If I am not much mistaken, a very general reaction was that if withdrawal from Northern Ireland was what the bombers wanted, then there must be something wrong with withdrawal from Northern Ireland. These bombings also had the effect in Britain of checking any vague tendencies to romanticize their perpetrators. Distance can lend enchantment to the view one may take of people like the IRA : in this case the bombings abolished the distance, and with it whatever enchantment it may have lent. The approval of the British public was in fact therefore assured for stronger anti-IRA policies both in Britain and Northern Ireland.

The general indifference of the British public towards Ireland, including Northern Ireland, has left British political leaders with a considerable degree of autonomy in dealing with Northern Irish matters. This is not an entirely reassuring reflection, since the same factors that confer the autonomy have often meant in the past, including the recent past, that politicians felt they need give the subject only intermittent and generally perfunctory attention. That is the kind of attention that is too impatient to be able to discern basic intractabilities, and is apt to imagine that it discerns brilliant short-cuts, fresh initiatives and the beginning of a solution where duller and more conventional minds see only the entry into yet another dangerous blind alley. I have seen eminent Englishmen in the grip of such bold visions and have tried in vain to pour cold water on the fire of their imaginations. I have talked—earnestly, but, as it proved, inaudibly—to Sir Harold Wilson on the day he saw the Provo leaders in Dublin and to Mr Whitelaw in London the day before *he* saw them.

I am opposed to British withdrawal from Northern Ireland and yet I have depicted British rule in Northern Ireland as having often been erratically shaped by the intermittent and therefore often ill-informed attention of the representatives of an indifferent British public. It will certainly be claimed that these positions are incompatible. If British rule rests on so unsound a basis, then surely it would be better if the British got out? The answer is: *not* surely. *British rule,* aspects of which I have described without sentimentality, *is far from ideal, but what might replace it might still be a lot worse.*

I shall come back to the British; but for the moment I want to turn to the Republic, and especially to the official policy of the Republic towards Northern Ireland.

In an address to the British-Irish Association last year at Oxford I discussed, on the basis of Father MacGréil's study *Prejudice and Tolerance in Ireland,* the subject of the attitudes of citizens of the Republic towards Northern Ireland. I shall of course not go over that ground again, but it is necessary to advert briefly here to surveys conducted since that time. These surveys on the whole confirm the picture which emerged from the MacGréil survey of a widely declared, but weakly held, aspiration towards unity in the Republic. A survey carried out by the Market Research Bureau of Ireland for the Dublin periodical *Magill* in September 1977 showed 63 per cent of its sample in the Republic as in favour of Irish unity. The 63 per cent was made up of 39 per cent as 'very much in favour', and 24 per cent as 'somewhat in favour'. Asked whether we should aim at unity whatever the problems, 33 per cent said yes; 32 per cent said only if the problems were not too great; and 18 per cent were all for unity provided it presented no problems at all. Predictably, the Dublin journalist who interpreted these figures saw them as showing 'an overwhelming majority in favour of the unity of Ireland . . . with a surprising depth of commitment to the idea'. The *Irish Press* commented that the poll showed 'a majority of the Irish believe we can run this country.' The poll of course was confined to the Republic.

In the Gallup poll carried out in the Republic for the BBC in March of this year [1978], one of the most striking features seems at first sight very encouraging. This is the figure of 76 per cent of respondents agreeing to the very sensible proposition that the people of Northern Ireland should be free to determine their own future. When one takes into account, however, that 69 per cent of respondents are in favour of the unity of Ireland (54 per cent as 'long-term' solution) and that (curiously) an even higher figure, 75 per cent, are in favour of British withdrawal, I think the inference is inescapable : that a significant proportion of that apparently sensible 76 per cent believe in the quite erroneous theory that the people of Northern Ireland would choose unity, if British withdrawal left them free to make the choice.

The Gallup poll shows 69 per cent in favour of unity but only 43 per cent as prepared to accept any form of extra taxation for the sake of Northern Ireland, while 51 per cent definitely rejected any extra taxation for that purpose. These figures are particularly interesting in view of recent nationalist suggestions that if the British public knew how much Northern Ireland was costing them in taxation they would vote to be relieved of the burden. So well they might : but if they did, it is fairly clear that the people of the Republic are far from anxious to take it up from them or, indeed, to accept any other burden for the sake of Northern Ireland. Nationalists would therefore be unwise, I think, to press the argument addressed to the British taxpayer since, in view of the attitude of taxpayers in the Republic, the unity aspired to and advocated would seem likely to involve a lowering of living standards in Northern Ireland.

The Gallup poll also brought out another point, significant I think of the degree of interest shown by the Republic in Northern Ireland. Of the respondents, 78 per cent had not been in Northern Ireland at any time in the last five years, and 50 per cent had never been there at all.

It is on an aspiration held with the degree of intensity implied by such responses that official policy in the Republic towards Northern Ireland—or, more exactly, towards the *question* of Northern Ireland—rests. That policy is in fact oriented not towards Northern Ireland but towards Britain. Britain is asked, in some way, to get Irish unity for us. Since it is agreed that unity is not to be attained without the consent of a majority in Northern Ireland, Britain must somehow get that consent. The first step—to quote the wording of its most recent formulation by a spokesman of the governing party in the Republic in a briefing to the Dublin political correspondents—is to be the obtaining of 'an indication from Britain of an interest in the ultimate unification of Ireland—the only long-term solution to the present crisis'.[1] Presumably this first step is to be followed by other steps, and one of these is supposed to be the withdrawal of British troops. A main plank in the policy of the governing party since 1975 has been the demand for a 'commitment by Britain to an orderly withdrawal from her involvement in the Six Counties of Northern Ireland'. The party has before now distinguished between its 'commitment' to withdraw and the Provos' declaration of intent, and has otherwise sought to remove any sense

[1] *Irish Times*, 16 June 1978.

of urgency from the concept of British withdrawal. In his briefing of the Dublin political correspondents on 15 June, however, the spokesman for the governing party goes further than he has ever done before in recognizing the dangers surrounding withdrawal. This in itself is greatly to be welcomed. In the briefing, the spokesman interpreted a call for a 'declaration of intent'—that is to say, as distinct from his party's 'commitment'—as, and I quote from the *Irish Times* account, 'a proposal to withdraw at a given time' from involvement in Northern Ireland affairs. That would mean the withdrawal of British forces, which he had always regarded, in present circumstances, as a dangerous move : I believe, said the spokesman, 'that that would be dangerous because, if a date were given—five, ten or fifteen years hence—there would be a possible build-up of preparedness by militants for that date. It would be disastrous if that happened.'

The spokesman did not explicitly say what that 'build-up of preparedness' is about, but his implication is quite clear : it would be a build-up of armed preparedness towards civil war.

*This is, I believe, the first time this danger has been recognized to this extent by the governing party.* Hitherto those of us who warned against that danger were dismissed as alarmist. The growth in realism here is to be welcomed in itself. However, a government policy which combines an unrealistic demand with a recognition of how dangerous that demand is cannot escape confusion, and the dangers which flow from confusion.

The British are to give a commitment to get out of Northern Ireland, but then they are to remain there indefinitely. At some point during that indefinite period they are to get the Unionists to agree to the unification of Ireland, and they are to do this in such a way that their withdrawal can be effected without danger of anything disastrous happening.

One of the odder aspects of this very odd policy is that it implies an extraordinary confidence in an extraordinary degree of skill, resolution, and continuity of policy to be manifested by an indefinite number of future successive British governments.

My own analysis of the British relation to Northern Ireland suggests that such expectations are without foundation. But my analysis is that of a person who is basically friendly to Britain. The present governing party in the Republic has as part of its political stock-in-trade the conception that British governments, however benign they may sound, have always 'let down Ireland' at every crucial moment: the 'Curragh mutiny' and Britain's failure to crush the Ulster Loyalists' strike of 1974 being obvious pertinent cases. If so, why should they imagine that it will be different in future? I don't think they do imagine anything of the kind. I don't think they imagine that the British can or will do anything so spectacularly unlikely as inducing Ulster Unionists to enter a United Ireland. But the policy of *'please say you're going, but for God's sake stay' has its advantages. It gives equivocal voice to equivocal aspirations. It* leaves Britain with the responsibility for Northern Ireland—indefinitely. It leaves the government of the Republic free to criticize Britain's discharge of those responsibilities—also indefinitely. This combination has a powerful, though unavowed, appeal to certain shrewd political minds. I infer, however, from the tone of the briefing from which I have just quoted, that the shrewd-

est of those minds has adverted to the danger that at
some point a British government may not only take him
at *his* word and say they are going, but may also then be
as good as their own word, and actually go—without
having previously performed the miracle of the political
conversion of the Northern Unionists into Republicans.
Departure in those circumstances would be, to use the
governing party's word, 'disastrous'. And not only for
Northern Ireland. The people and institutions of the Republic would be among the prime victims of any such
disaster.

Britain's commitment to Northern Ireland is reluctant,
and on the part of the British public unwanted : the attention of the British Government to Northern Irish
affairs is intermittent, and has often been miscalculated.
As for the Republic, *most of its citizens know and care
little more about the realities of Northern Ireland than
do those of Great Britain* and its Government's present
policies are astutely adapted not for acquiring responsibility but for avoiding it in a manner acceptable to the
Republic's citizens, who are not hypercritical in such
matters. Northern Ireland is constitutionally part of the
United Kingdom and is also the subject of an appropri-
ately ambiguous constitutional claim from the Republic.
It appears to be contended for, but in reality the contention between the democracies is rather less than half-
hearted on both sides.

Yet this strange and almost ghostly contention is
fraught with deep danger. By the uncertainties, hopes
and fears which it creates, it tends to exacerbate the
antagonisms between the communities in Northern Ireland, and to sustain an atmosphere propitious to violence.
This brings me in, from London and from Dublin, right

here to Belfast, to discuss in the concluding part of my address some of the realities of this province, as seen by an interested and concerned outsider. I know how futile it is for such an outsider to address advice, warnings, pleas or exhortations to either community—or, if you prefer that language, either section of the community—in Northern Ireland. It so happens, however, that a very able leader of one community, Mr Austin Currie, in an article published in this city ten days ago[1] rebuked me, in very civil language, for not having asked, 'never mind answered', what Mr Currie calls 'the fundamental question'. As framed by Mr Currie, that question is: 'If para-militaries ended their violence tomorrow, what changes should be made to ensure there will not be a further and probably worse outbreak in five, ten or fifteen years?'

There the question is: if I did not ask it, I have at least now publicly repeated it, after Mr Currie. I shall now not merely answer it, but answer it twice over, once as framed by Mr Currie, and once as I would frame it myself.

The answer to the question as framed by Mr Currie is short:

'None. There are no changes that can be made that will ensure an end to violence now, or ensure the prevention of the recurrence of violence at any future time.' In general terms there is no known means of ensuring the elimination of violence from any society. Specifically as regards Northern Ireland, there are no conceivable changes that will simultaneously appease and disarm *both* those who passionately endeavour to break the connection with Great Britain, and those who equally

[1] Review-article 'Stimulating reading Dr O'Brien, but there is one question you haven't asked', *Belfast Telegraph*, 13 June 1978.

passionately oppose that endeavour. The idea that there exists *some way of half-breaking the connection* that will do the trick *is an illusion*!

That last proposition ought to be self-evident, but I can quite see why it is not. It is not self-evident because it is so desolatingly devoid of all comfort. We all find it hard to accept bad news even when it is true. Yet stubborn refusal to accept a self-evident proposition necessarily leads to absurdities, and absurdities have a tendency to make the unacceptable bad news even worse than it was before. The worst of it is that it is men of goodwill who have the greatest tendency to flinch from this self-evidence, thereby producing a kind of intellectual paralysis at the very point where intellectual vigour is most needed. It is not here Yeats's case of the best lacking all conviction while the worst are full of passionate intensity. The worst are up to specification all right, but with the best it is now a case of losing, through compassion, the power to think, and in consequence acquiring convictions of an irrational character, either irrelevant or damaging to those whom they seek to help, nor is this tendency confined to us Irish. Indeed Englishmen of goodwill, wishing to think about Ireland in a positive way, are peculiarly susceptible to this disease. One sees this in the media, but not only there. I found, with a mixture of amusement and horror, a notable symptom of this particular trouble in the very interesting memoirs of a distinguished and amiable man, having held high responsibilities in Anglo-Irish affairs. The memoirs are those of Sir John Peck, the predecessor of Christopher Ewart-Biggs as Ambassador to Dublin. At the end of Sir John's important narrative—which should be read by all who are interested in British-Irish relations

—he casts around for some initiatives which would be likely to end IRA violence. The main device he comes up with is the creation of an Anglo-Irish Council. Now how, I wonder, would those whose proclaimed objective is to break the connection between England and Ireland be mollified by the existence of an Anglo-Irish Council?

The main changes which Mr Currie and his friends—including Mr Lynch—have in mind, are the re-creation of some kind of power-sharing executive and some recognition of the Irish dimension—the resurrection, in fact, of Sunningdale. Now *Sunningdale was a brave endeavour*, and one in which I am proud to have taken part, *but it failed.* One reason why it failed was it could not ensure in the present what it aimed at bringing about ultimately—peace. Now, while the advantages of Sunningdale were obvious for Catholics, all it appeared to offer to the Protestants was the promise of peace—which they saw primarily as the end of IRA activity. When Provos blew the heart out of Royal Avenue, there was nothing positive left in Sunningdale from a Protestant point of view. The Protestant attack on Sunningdale was based on a strong feeling that it was conceived as a step towards Irish unity. The leader of those Protestants who participated in Sunningdale, the late Brian Faulkner, protested that this was quite wrong: there was no question of Irish unity involved in Sunningdale. He and his party associates were good Unionists. It was absolutely vital for the success of Sunningdale that Mr Faulkner should be believed. But how could he be believed when important Catholic and nationalist participants in Sunningdale, and also the Dublin media, could be heard saying publicly, with complacency and in some cases a note of triumphalism, that a step to unity was just what it was? The belief among Protestants that that indeed *was* just what it was, was what destroyed Sunningdale, through the support available to the Loyalist strike—support by no means all of which was due to intimidation.

The noises made in favour of a new Sunningdale—though that ominous name is not used—show that those concerned have learned nothing from the Sunningdale experience. They still associate the call for power sharing with the call for progress towards unity, and they are then surprised when Unionists, being by definition opposed to the unification of Ireland, and having seen the fate of the Faulkner Unionists, will not talk power sharing. They complain of unionist intransigence. But when there were 'intransigent unionists', Sunningdale unionists, around, what did those who complain now about intransigence do? They undermined the Sunningdale unionists, and helped the intransigent ones by talking incessantly about unity. Now, faced with the intransigence they helped to fortify, they look to Britain to overcome that intransigence. But how can that be? If—as Brian Faulkner for one believed—all the Queen's horses and all the Queen's men stood idly by, that phrase again, when the Sunningdale Humpty Dumpty was pushed off the wall, how are these forces then supposed to succeed in their proverbially impossible task of putting Humpty together again?

Let me then rephrase Mr Currie's question as follows:

'What should be done now which would be likely steadily to promote and maintain better relations between the two communities, progressively isolate the men of violence in both communities, and thereby create the conditions most favourable for reducing violence to a minimum?'

My short answer to that is : *'Give direct rule a chance.'* That is advice which I think should be directed towards both communities, preferably by people with influence in each.

From both communities there has been some effort to replace direct rule. I have discussed the efforts of leading representatives of the Catholic community. Coming from sections of the Protestant community, three alternatives to direct rule have been proposed. One is an independent Northern Ireland. As that appears to lack any widespread support *at present*, I shall forbear from discussing the disasters which would, I believe, attend on that particular 'solution'. I would suggest to Catholics, however, that they should keep carefully in mind what might be in store for them under majority rule in an independent Northern Ireland. They should also take note of the fact that, if direct rule does come to an end, the successor regime is very much more likely to be an independent Northern Ireland than a united Ireland. If they think along these lines—as probably many of them already silently do—they will I think see that there is more to be said for direct rule, and more danger involved in undermining it, than their representatives at present like to acknowledge.

The second Protestant alternative to direct rule is the restoration of Stormont : both communities tend to be restoration-minded. Mr Paisley's strike in 1977 put support for that to the test. The failure of that strike suggests that while most Protestants probably would prefer such a restoration to direct rule, the preference is not of such an intensity as to disrupt the life of the Province—at least to anything like the extent to which it would be likely to be disrupted by Catholic reaction to that particular restoration.

The third Protestant alternative, and the one now most canvassed, is what is called integration. In practice, it appears that integration means no more than a continuation of direct rule combined with increasing Northern Ireland's representation at Westminster to a level proportionate to its population. To the *substance* of that I see no objection. The trouble is in the word—and the intent behind the word—'integration'. In the state of relations between the two communities in Northern Ireland, and since integration has been made a dirty word among many Catholics, the coming of integration would be seen, and would I fear be presented, as a goal scored by the Prods against the Micks—just as the desiderated British 'indication of interest' in Irish unity, which sounds equally innocuous, would be seen and presented as a goal or a series of goals scored by the Micks against the Prods. Either goal would be followed by a hullabaloo among the fans favourable to violence, and in no way propitious for reconciliation.

Northern Ireland needs no more of such goal-scoring, and one of the great merits of direct rule is that it does not provide much of a stadium for this kind of football. It has other merits, which ought to be obvious, but do not always seem to be. Granted the present and long-standing relation between the two communities, direct rule is the least intolerable of possible forms of government for the Province. Neither community admits to liking it, and that reaction in both communities is a predictable characteristic of any solution which is not totally unacceptable to one or other of the communities. From the point of view of the *Protestant* community, direct rule has at least the *merit of protecting* the *basic allegiance of that community to the connection with Britain.* From the point of view of most Catholics—though not of course of the IRA—direct rule has the merit of removing from Northern Ireland the political institutions of Protestant supremacy and Catholic inferiority. These are not inconsiderable merits, and I see no other available form of rule which comes near to matching either their balance or their solidity. I should add that there may well be much more support for direct rule among ordinary people of both communities, than might be inferred from the public statements of their representatives.

How solid can we regard direct rule itself as being? Earlier in this address, and by design, I stressed inherent weaknesses in Britain's connection with Northern Ireland, and therefore also in this system of rule. I stressed the British public's negative feelings with regard to the connection, and the intermittent and sometimes damaging attention which British governments have conferred on it. From this you might infer that direct rule is a fragile plant, not likely to live long. But there are other factors, which I have left over until now, which indicate that *direct rule* might not be so fragile, and may have quite a long life before it. A main factor is that British politicians, while they have made quite as many mistakes in this matter as Irish ones, have shown a much greater capacity than the Irish ones to learn from their mistakes. This is not because the British are more pragmatic—it would be hard to imagine a more pragmatic politician than Mr Lynch—but because British governments, of both parties, have had experience of the consequences of mistakes and have had the responsibility of dealing with these consequences. They have, for example, I believe, ceased to toy with the idea of finding some compromise formula which will make the Provos so happy that they voluntarily give up killing and burning. They have had, and have taken, the opportunity to measure the dimensions of the disaster which would occur if Britain withdrew from Northern Ireland while relations between the two communities remain as they are now. The danger is of course that of civil war, which would engulf the whole island of Ireland.

They know that such a disaster in the neighbouring island could not but have repercussions—including international repercussions—exceedingly damaging to Great Britain itself.

For these reasons I believe that despite the vague dissatisfaction of the British public, British governments, now better informed than their public, will persist in direct rule—with or without increased representation—for quite a long time to come. Mr Lynch says British withdrawal will occur 'ultimately'. Of course ultimately all human arrangements have to come to an end. Without quibbling about that, *it seems reasonably clear that a long period of direct rule should be expected.* It is argued that this period should be used for the building of agreed institutions in Northern Ireland which will ensure peace and order after British departure. Ideally, yes. Unfortunately, at the present time, no such agreement is in sight. To seek to bring about such agreement by pressure on the representatives of one community can only worsen ill-feeling and widen disagreement between the communities. This is surely the wrong way of proceeding. The effort at the present time should not be to attempt things which the communities are not agreed to do. There should rather be an effort to identify areas, however narrow, of unforced agreement : by working in these areas to seek to widen them, and so gradually to establish such working relations between the two communities as will permit—at that stage—the building of stable agreed political institutions, such as would allow British troops to be withdrawn without untoward consequences. It is most certainly not possible now for the two communities to agree on constitutional arrangements, and the effort to concentrate the dialogue on such arrangements is profoundly misguided. Can any significant degree of inter-community agreement be found to work on such problems, for example, that of unemployment, which should be of concern to all, regardless of religion or allegiance? Could agreement be found for both sets of leaders to seek investment in Northern Ireland without political strings attached? Could there be at least a tacit recognition, among community leaders, of direct rule as a present necessity, and of the need to use the period of direct rule for binding up the wounds of this gravely injured province, and not for giving a further airing to claims and counter-claims that helped to cause these wounds?

It will be said that, with the best will in the world, these things cannot even be discussed : there is no forum in which to discuss them. But there *could* be such a forum : the idea of a Consultative Assembly to advise the Secretary of State has been mooted. It could work best if its terms of reference confined it to the internal affairs of the Province, with an emphasis on social and economic matters. Such an Assembly would certainly come into being if representatives of the two communities were to agree to it. If agreement cannot yet be found even on such a matter—which surely threatens nobody—then it is obviously premature to talk about finding agreement on matters which have been the objects of long, bitter and sterile contention.

I have said that *direct rule should be given a chance.* Britain can help to give it a chance, by recognizing clearly that there is no present or early alternative to it, and seeking to apply it *creatively* and with *consultation in the social and economic spheres.* In turn, direct rule gives a chance to the people of Northern Ireland. It is only the people of Northern Ireland themselves who can determine how that chance will be used. That choice is theirs alone. They cannot get agreement among themselves by looking outside for it.

The chances of any agreement at all in the near future seem very slim. But if we assume, as I do, that direct rule will be there for a long time, then the important thing in the present and near future, is to avoid actions and language which would prejudice a slow *rapprochement* and possible agreement or accommodation at a later date. If that does not happen, then either direct rule continues indefinitely or we or our children will have to face the *dire consequences of British withdrawal in the continuing absence of any agreement* between the Northern Ireland communities. Those consequences would profoundly affect all Ireland, and these islands generally. To recognize that now, and to observe the prudence its recognition dictates, is the only means by which we can hope to avoid such an eventual disaster.

I have addressed you in this way as part of a continued

effort to encourage such a recognition, and to dispel some of the clouds of illusion which impede its emergence. I intend to continue that effort as long as it is necessary, or as long as life permits, whichever may be the shorter.

# 3

## Ireland, Britain, America

*Delivered at New York University,*
*30 November 1978*

To call in the New World to redress the balance of the
old was a phrase coined by a British statesman. It came
to apply to the main aim of British policy in the opening
phases of two World Wars.

To call on Americans of Irish decent to redress the
balance of the British Isles was, in substance, the main
aim of the international activity of Irish nationalists since
the end of the American Civil War. I say in substance
because the formula I used is not itself a nationalist one :
for true Irish nationalists there are no British Isles and
never were any. There is only Ireland and England, an
eternal Manichean duality. Scotland and Wales may,
indeed, be made out too, but dimly and doubtfully. Are
they, too, nationalities oppressed by England, rightly
struggling to be free? Irish nationalists tend to take that
view in public, on appropriate occasions and at Pan-
Celtic congresses. In private they admit to doubts. The
Scots and the Welsh may be struggling rightly, but they
don't seem to be struggling very hard. Also, they are
Protestants, like the English, and while Irish nationalists
profess to hold that religion is altogether irrelevant to

their politics, they know in their hearts that the nation of
their nationalism is Catholic Ireland, to which Scottish
Presbyterians and Welsh Nonconformists—when they
have to be seen in that light—are hardly less alien than
the English. There is a further difficulty, never explicitly
formulated but obscurely sensed. The difficulty turns
on the Irish nationalist axiom of sacral insularity: the
theory, assumed to be a self-evident truth, that an island
is inherently a permanent political unit, to divide which
is unnatural and unjust. But if this principle is indeed
self-evident, how can it be right for Scotland and Wales,
parts of an island, to be independent?

Scotland and Wales are grey areas ... intellectually
exhausting and emotionally unsatisfactory. It is a relief
to get back to just Ireland and England, the eternal right
versus the eternal wrong:

> *On our side is virtue and Erin*
> *On theirs is the Saxon and guilt*

And again:

> *The rose shall fade*
> *And the shamrock shine forever new*

Few nationalists today would use such tropes without
some kind of smile, yet the dualism which they represent
is deep-rooted in nationalism. Irish nationalism defined
itself, of necessity, *against* England as well as *for* Ireland,
and Irish nationalists even today tend to think of the
'against' as the critical test of the 'for'. I say 'tend'; in
Ireland today the tendency is, for most people, rather
hesitant, intermittent and ambiguous. Those who can
feel they hate their living neighbours, the actual English
of the present day, are clearly a very small minority in-

deed. The MacGréil survey of the social attitudes of Dubliners, carried out in 1972, revealed the rather remarkable fact that English people are not only acceptable to Dubliners—in the basic sense of being welcome into their families—but that they are more acceptable than people of any other nationality, including Americans, and more acceptable also than Northern Irish people. On the acceptability scale :

| | |
|---|---|
| English | 89% |
| Northern Irish | 78% |
| Americans | 69% |

Though the survey was carried out only in Dublin, it is not likely that the proportions would be widely different for the whole Republic, since so many Dubliners are of recent rural origin. Yet, though feelings towards English people are so overwhelmingly positive, there is a significant minority—including some of those who like the English people—who hate England, at least in the abstract. In the 1972 survey, 17.1 per cent of respondents said they 'would like to see England brought to its knees'. Moreover, it appears that this significant minority of haters has the uneasy respect of a much larger minority. A Gallup poll carried out in the Republic this year [1978] for the BBC showed that while only a tiny minority— 2 per cent—actually approved of the Provisional IRA campaign of violence, a large minority—35 per cent— attributed idealistic motives to the Provisionals, and expressed respect for these. True, a majority of the whole sample condemned the Provisionals absolutely, but it was the smallest majority possible : 51 per cent. Like all who belong to that rather precarious majority, I have to be deeply concerned about that 35 per cent.

That 35 per cent, who condemn what the IRA do,

while respecting motives which they attribute to them, form a significant element in the political culture of modern Ireland, and explain much that seems ambivalent in the attitudes of Church and State towards political violence.

To the eyes of that large ambivalent minority, the IRA appear, in a dim and uneasy light, as the executors and executants of the legacy of the past. They are subconsciously perceived as a kind of Furies, charged with a punitive mission of archaic legitimacy. They ought to be dissuaded and if necessary, prevented, from carrying out that mission, but the dissuasion or prevention should be accompanied by at least an implicit deference, a touch of awe before the antique source of the abhorred deed. One of the most representative and respected Irishmen alive, Dr Cathal Daly, Bishop of Ardagh and Clonmacnoise, condemns violence with passionate sincerity, and yet in the same breath praises the idealism of those who do the deed he condemns. Hearing or reading the Bishop's words, I have known moments, and longer than moments, of impatience with that good and gentle man. The 'idealism' has seemed to be attributed to the killers on rather scanty evidence, and to serve as a veil covering more obvious and repellant characteristics. Yet, when I fit that cryptic word 'idealist', to the notion of the punitive executant of an archaically legitimate mission, I find myself equipped not merely to understand the Bishop's message, but to respect it profoundly. The Bishop is speaking as a Christian priest to people who are nominally Christians, but whose morality is really attached to the more gorily tribalist parts of the Old Testament, transferred of course to a different tribe from that originally chosen. But the Bishop, and those grisly audi-

tors of his, have also their archetypes, as I have suggested, not only among the Judaic but also among the
Hellenic origins of our civilization. In essentials, and
very precisely, the message is that of the Goddess
Athena, at the end of the *Oresteia* of Aeschylus, to the
Eumenides who came to wreak vengeance on Orestes.
She tells them that their mission is legitimate, on the
terms which they have inherited, but that its execution
has ceased to be legitimate. Under the new dispensation,
the blood-cycle of vengeance must end. Provided they
accept that, the Eumenides are entitled to be respected
and to have a temple in the city. That, it seems to me, is
what the Bishop means too: to soothe the sacred ser-
pents, and to draw their poisoned fangs. It seems worth
trying, particularly as an accompaniment to more conventional forms of law-enforcement.

Much of this must seem, to some of you at least, oddly
fanciful, and certainly very remote from contemporary
America. Fanciful I agree it is. I also think that fancy, the
exercise of the imagination, may be necessary to the
understanding of these matters. One can err—as I have
often erred—not indeed by being 'too logical', as is often
said, but by being insufficiently curious, imaginatively
speaking, about the partly hidden historically-con-
ditioned emotional premises from which reasoning in
political and social matters has to proceed. As regards
contemporary America, it cannot be *entirely* contemporary, or even as contemporary as it consciously thinks of
itself: the New World carries the old world, and even
the ancient world, within itself. Specifically that part of
America which concerns itself with Ireland, carries
within itself a version of the old country: a version that
is often closer to the creed of our Eumenides, the archaic

legitimacy of righteous hatred and revenge, than is any version now widely prevalent in the old country itself.

But how large is the part of America that does concern itself with Ireland, and how intensely does it concern itself with that country? As far as I know, these questions cannot be answered by reference to any precise data. Modern techniques for surveying public opinion by weighted samples work no doubt reasonably well—provided you know what you are taking a sample *of*. Dubliners, the residents of the city of Dublin, are an identifiable population, whose opinions may be elicited, with a fairly small margin of error. But neither 'Americans concerned with Ireland' nor—what is generally assumed to be the same thing—'Irish Americans' form such an identifiable population. There are some politicians with Irish names who sometimes claim to speak for Irish-Americans, and there are other politicians *without* Irish names who try to speak *to* those whom the first lot claim to speak *for*. The second lot tend to use an even more exuberant version of the language used by the first lot, no doubt on the theory that what is said by somebody with an Irish name must be congenial to other people with Irish names. I have found by personal experiment, both in Ireland and in America, that this theory is not invariably borne out by the facts.

Some thirty years ago, when I worked in what was then the Department of External Affairs in Dublin, we had no difficulty in identifying who were the Irish-Americans, or Americans of Irish origin to use the preferred phrase, how many of them there were, and exactly what they thought of Ireland. There were thirty million of them and whenever they were mentioned, what they were found to be thinking was in gratifying accord with

63

whatever the Government of Dublin wanted to think of them as thinking. When I entered the Department, the late and great Eamon de Valera was Minister of External Affairs as well as Taoiseach. One of his most famous sayings—to which indeed his career lent much justification —was to the effect that when he wished to know what the people of Ireland thought he looked into his own heart. With much less justification we, his official servants, were applying to a distant and dimly discernible population the master's technique of cognition through cardiac introspection.

Yet in this matter, as in others, it is possible also to push agnosticism too far. We cannot know how many Americans there are who feel an emotional bond to Ireland, or to a version of Irish history, but we do know that Americans in that category have exerted a powerful, and at times a fateful, influence over the history of Ireland and, through Ireland, of Britain, and that they continue to exert a significant, though diminished, influence in our own day. The nature of that influence was determined by their double experience, first in rural Ireland under British political and landlord social rule, and then in America as poor emigrants. The first element has often been emphasized to the exclusion of the second, and therefore over-emphasized. Evelyn Waugh wrote of the Irish as bringing with them to America 'their ancient rancours and the melancholy of the bogs'. They did that; after all they had, in the nineteenth century, quite a lot to be rancorous and quite a lot to be melancholy about. Irish Catholics had been for centuries a conquered, stigmatized suspect minority in an archipelago dominated by Protestant England. I am using the terms 'Catholic' and 'Protestant' because these are the basic terms of the discussion.

The term 'the Irish', as generally used, both in Ireland and outside it refers to Irish Catholics. Most generalizations about 'the Irish' apply, and are felt to apply, to Irish Catholics, and not to Ulster Protestants. I am referring here to ordinary, everyday spontaneous usage. There is another usage, a careful, on-your-best-behaviour usage, according to which 'the Irish' are spoken of, and supposed to be thought of, as including the Ulster Protestants. The Irish Republican tradition formally inculcates this usage, and it is official doctrine in the Republic of Ireland. This is a 'musical bank' usage in the sense of Butler's *Erewhon*. It can only be made to work in carefully prepared discourses; when the speaker is off his guard, or under stress of emotion, the natural usage—the coinage of the *real* bank—comes into circulation. Thus the phrase 'our people in the North' is one that has been heard very often from speakers in the Republic over the past ten years. According to the official doctrine, formally professed by all these speakers, 'our people in the North' should mean all the people of Northern Ireland, both Catholic and Protestant, joined together by Wolfe Tone's common name of 'Irishman'. But the phrase 'our people in the North' was never used in that sense and never understood in that sense. It always referred, and was always instinctively understood to refer, exclusively to the Catholics of Northern Ireland. The others, the Ulster Protestants, are not felt to be 'our people' any more than they, as a collectivity, feel themselves to be 'our people' —in the sense of making up one people with the Catholics of the Republic. That is why the island of Ireland is divided.

In modern times, the interaction between Ireland and America has hinged on an interaction of Catholics—Irish Catholics at home in Ireland and descendants of Irish Catholics in the United States. That interaction, during the past hundred years, has had momentous effects. From the 1880s on, it played a major part in the destruction of the Irish landlord system, and its replacement by a system of small farmers among their own land. That was the major *social* revolution to occur in Ireland in modern times : more fundamental and more significant in human terms than the purely political revolution of the twentieth century. But that nineteenth-century social revolution was also implicitly and proleptically a political revolution. The nature of this revolution, and the determinant role of the American Irish in it, were discerned by a British Home Secretary: 'In former Irish rebellions', wrote Sir William Harcourt, 'the Irish were *in* Ireland. We could reach their forces, cut off their resources in men and money, and then to subjugate was comparatively easy. Now there is an Irish nation in the United States, equally hostile, with plenty of money, absolutely beyond our reach and yet within ten days' sail of our shore. No government could carry on such a war with a divided opinion in Britain.' Harcourt was writing on Christmas Eve, 1885, and what he was explaining was the inevitability of Home Rule. He was right about that. Where he and his leader, Gladstone, were wrong was in the assumption that the unit for Home Rule—and eventually, as it proved, for independence—had to be the island of Ireland. When Harcourt wrote of 'the Irish', he meant—like almost everyone else using this term—the Catholic Irish. They were the ones who wanted Home Rule, and eventually got independence. What British Liberals and Catholic Irish alike agreed to regard as insignificant was the existence of a body of people in Ireland—the Ulster Protestants—who not merely did not want Home Rule, but absolutely refused to have it.

Protestant Ulster proved to be the rock on which both the British Liberal Party and the Irish Nationalist Party —the Home Rule Partners—struck and foundered. Ulster Protestants armed to resist Home Rule, Irish Catholics armed to insist on Home Rule and—later—on a sovereign independent Republic of all Ireland. The Catholics claimed to have no intention of coercing the Protestants. But in fact their programme, being an all-Ireland one, and being rejected by Protestant Ulster, was unrealizable unless *someone*—Liberal England or Catholic Ireland—could and would coerce Protestant Ulster. The leaders of the 1916 Rising had been supporters of Home Rule and regarded England as having betrayed Home Rule by failing to ensure that it would apply to all Ireland—by failing, that is, though the complaint was never so formulated, to coerce Protestant Ulster. The heirs of the 1916 Rising—Sinn Fein and the armed forces nominally responsible to it—reasserted the doctrine of all-Ireland separatism. Although this continued to imply the coercion of Protestant Ulster—the implication being of course still denied—the actual fighting was directed at the British forces. The British, having rightly declined to coerce Protestant Ulster, for a time in 1919–21 tried their hands at coercing Catholic Ireland. This attempt at coercion failed for precisely the reasons diagnosed by Harcourt in rejecting coercion thirty-five years before: American support for 'the Irish', and divided opinion in Britain itself.

The dual rejection by Britain of coercion either from Catholic Ireland or Protestant Ulster necessitated partition. Many writers on the subject have found this obvious fact so unpalatable that they have written as if it did not exist—as if, that is, Britain disposed of, but neglected to use, some means, other than coercion, of inducing Ulster Protestants to leave a State in which they wished to remain, and enter a State which they did not wish to enter. What this means of inducement might be, I have nowhere seen clearly stated, although the phantom of its putative existence haunts this whole controversy, and regularly clanks its chains in the editorial columns of the newspapers of the Republic. Some British liberal writers, with a credulity perhaps derived from a sense of guilt, have tried to accredit this phenomenon. Mr George Dangerfield, for example, both in *The Strange Death of Liberal England* and more recently in *The Damnable Question* has written, in an engaging style, to suggest that the partition of Ireland was caused by the weakness of English Liberals and the wickedness of English Tories, and not by the will of a million Ulster Protestants. That is an extraordinarily superficial historical judgement, and one that leads to dangerous delusions. If those delusions are widely prevalent, both in Ireland and even, though to a lesser extent, in Britain, it is not surprising that they should take on an even more extreme form three thousand miles away, in this country. I have heard a prominent Irish-American politician, of this city, only a few years ago, 'explaining' Northern Ireland to a radio audience. All the violence, he explained, was caused by British imperialism. 'What', his interviewer asked, 'about the Ulster Protestants?' The Protestants, said the politician blandly, were fine people who would make a magnificent contribution to a united Ireland. The interviewer wanted to know what was keeping these Protestants from making this contribution? The answer was that Britain was keeping them. Britain, and Britain alone, was preventing the Ulster Protestants from entering a united Ireland.

This fantasy, proceeding from a brain oppressed by the Irish Republican version of history, is of course one that legitimizes the IRA campaign in Northern Ireland. If it is Britain that keeps Ireland divided, then Ireland can be united by shooting British soldiers and British officials. In the belief that the proposition about British responsibility was true, the men who killed Christopher Ewart-Biggs saw their act as justified. Responsible leaders of opinion in the Republic condemned them. But what right exactly had they to condemn them? Some of them are a people who accepted the fantastic premises about the origin of partition, but shrank from the conclusion to which those premises pointed. Their condemnation was humane and decent but indicative of intellectual disaster. There are also those who know well enough that it is not Britain that keeps Ireland divided, but do not hold it expedient to say so and even find it expedient, on occasion, to suggest the reverse of that which they know. In their case the disaster was not intellectual but moral. Both sets of disasters had helped to set the scene for the deadly act.

So had corresponding disasters in America, whence the organization of the obsessed assassins has drawn most of its money. It would appear that support for that organization, the IRA, has been stronger among Americans of Irish origin than among Irish people living in Ireland. Such support, of course, depends on the inten-

sity of anti-British feeling. As I indicated earlier, the
feelings of the Irish in Ireland about the British are
ambiguous and include, along with some intense hostil-
ity, much more widespread friendly feelings. Public-
opinion surveys enable us, in Ireland, to keep track of
these patterns, of these feelings, and of the contradictions
within them, in a certain amount of detail. Unfortunately, it would be difficult, perhaps impossible, to carry
out equivalent studies among Irish-Americans, because
of the difficulty in identifying the population to be surveyed. That famous figure of thirty million to which I
referred earlier, was based, I believe, on an estimate of
how many Americans had one Irish grandparent. Apart
from the possibility that the grandparent might have
been a Presbyterian from Portadown, it is clear enough
that many of those so descended will not have any strong
sense of identification with Ireland or interest in its
politics. Yet it is also clear, historically, that many Americans of Irish origin—even if we cannot know how many
—have had such a strong identification and such an interest. Many Irish people, living in Ireland, have tended
in this century to see the anti-Britishness of Irish-Americans as excessive, and to relate it to the time and circumstances of the emigration of the ancestors. Most of those
ancestors left at times, in the middle and late nineteenth
centuries, when the oppressive power of the landlord
was a very real thing, and was backed and maintained
by the forces of the British Crown. Certainly, if one's
vision of Ireland and Britain is of *that* Ireland and *that*
Britain, one is likely to feel more anti-British than if one
has contemporary realities in the forefront of one's mind.

Yet it has not just been a matter of brooding on the
past. In American conditions, for Irish Catholic emi-

grants, Irish nationalism had a functional utility. Initially
despised because of their poverty and their Catholicity,
their most vocal spokesman laid hold, almost instinctively, on what might be called the Americanism of their
Irishness. The Irish who fought against England were
carrying on, in the eighteenth and nineteenth centuries,
the same struggle as the American revolutionaries. The
American-Irish, writes William V. Shannon, 'defined
themselves not only as Americans but as Americans of a
superpatriotic kind, and as proof they offered the fact of
their Irishness and their devotion to old Ireland'. The
same writer goes on to quote a fairly characteristic expression, by Patrick Ford of the *Irish World*, a little over
a hundred years ago, of the American version of Irish
nationalism : 'Here in this Republic—whose flag first
fluttered on the breeze in defiance of England—whose
first national hosts rained an iron hail of destruction upon
England's power—here in this land to whose shores England's oppression exiled our race—we are free to express
the sentiments and declare the hopes of Ireland.' The
implication of the concluding passage of that is particularly interesting : it is that the American-Irish, being
free to speak in the land of the free, constitute the
authentic voice of Ireland, whereas the representatives
of the Irish in Ireland do not. That same claim is heard
today, from American supporters of the IRA, wherever
the representatives of successive Dublin governments
condemn that body in the name of Ireland. Ireland, these
supporters feel, is alive and living in America.

Accentuated anti-Britishness has been a weapon of
Americans of Irish descent, both in their social and political struggles. I myself heard, about ten years ago on a
pavement in the Bronx, a highly pertinent conversation

between two small boys. The younger one wanted to know what was the difference between the Republicans and the Democrats. The older boy told him : 'The Democrats are up for the Americans. The Republicans are up for the British.'

I have no doubt as to the ethnicity of the boy who gave that answer.

The social functions served by accentuated anti-Britishness have probably largely been discharged, but habits tend to outlive functions. The habit of seeing Irishness in terms of anti-Britishness is still fairly strong, and hurts Ireland more than it hurts Britain.

It may be said that I have laid too much stress upon the past, not enough upon a struggle now proceeding. Also—and relatedly—I have talked about Ulster Protestants. What about Ulster Catholics? Are they not an oppressed people, are the IRA not trying to liberate them, and are these freedom-fighters not entitled to American support?

The Catholics of Northern Ireland have been the principal victims of the Home Rule and anti-Home-Rule struggles, and of the consequent political division of the British Isles and of Ireland. The system of devolved democratic government in Northern Ireland left the Catholics in a permanent minority, governed by representatives of a majority which felt itself to be besieged by Catholics. In these conditions, Catholics were discriminated against in housing and jobs and in the local franchise. They were also humiliated, by certain ritual commemorative ceremonies and in other ways.

Directly, the Catholics were the victims of local forms of Protestant intolerance. Against Britain itself—that is, against successive British governments—three main

charges can justly be made. Not the charge of creating
partition: that was inevitable. The real charges are:
drawing the boundary line in such a way as to include in
Northern Ireland more Catholics than was equitable or
necessary; setting up devolved government, in conditions in which this could only mean rule by one community over the other; and thirdly the systematic ignor-
ing by Westminster of the workings of Northern Ireland
devolution up to the time when the Civil Rights movement among Catholics, and Protestant reactions to that
movement, forced the situation upon the attention of the
British public.

The Provisional IRA from the beginning of the seven-
ties moved in to exploit that situation. Their object has
not been, and is not, just or mainly the liberation of
Catholics, but the unification of Ireland first by elimination of the British seen as 'responsible for partition',
and then by coercion of the Protestants. The people who
have suffered most, and are placed in most danger, by
the IRA campaign and by its objectives, are the Catholics
of Northern Ireland. They have endured intimidation by
the IRA itself and retaliation by the enemies of the IRA.
If the IRA were successful in bringing about British withdrawal, the outcome would not be a united Ireland, or
the liberation of Catholics, but an independent Pro-
testant-dominated Northern Ireland, in which the fate
of Catholics would be likely to be far worse than the
worst they had to endure under devolution.

Today, devolved government has gone, and with it
all forms of State discrimination against Catholics. Surveys show that experience of direct rule from Britain,
replacing Stormont devolution, has developed a high
degree of acceptability in both communities, and a much

higher degree of such acceptability than any other proffered 'solution'. Broadly, it is acceptable to Protestants
because it is an expression of the Union with Britain,
with which they have been identified over many generations, and it is acceptable to Catholics because it replaces
discriminatory devolution by impartial State processes.
It is not anyone's ideal, but nothing better is even re-
motely in sight. It gives time for the reduction of fear,
resentment and suspicion. It provides a framework
within which, with luck, and in the absence of untoward
external intervention, the two communities may begin
to find better ways of living together.

The fact of the acceptability of direct rule, obvious
though it is, is in itself unacceptable to many. It is unacceptable because it goes against the grain of the version of Irish history handed down to Irish Catholics and
to their descendants in this country, as well as to their
sympathizers in other countries. It went against that
same grain for me to move towards this conclusion, and
to form the opinions expressed in this lecture. I did so—
as many have done in all countries—by having to think
again, in the light of contemporary events, about a received interpretation of history. Such re-thinking is pain-
ful enough, both in itself and in its effects, if the history
in question is that of one's own people, and a history in
which one's own family played a certain part.

It so happens—and not without irony—that I am the
third member of my family, in three successive generations, to come to America to talk about Ireland and about
Britain, and how Americans should look at these.

The first was my great-uncle, Father Eugene Sheehy,
known as 'the Land League priest', who came to this
country with Charles Stewart Parnell in the spring of

1880, to raise funds for the agrarian revolution and for the Home Rule cause—an effort whose fateful implications were discerned by Home Secretary Harcourt five years later, in a passage which I quoted.

The second was Father Eugene's niece, my mother's eldest sister, Hanna Sheehy-Skeffington, who came to this country some thirty-six years later, in the aftermath of the Dublin Rising of 1916. Her husband, the pacifist, socialist, and feminist Francis Sheehy-Skeffington, had been taken as a hostage during the Rising. He was shot to death on the order of a British officer, of Anglo-Irish origin, who was later charged with murder and found guilty, but insane. Hanna came here to speak about that experience, and against British imperialism, as part of an effort to keep America out of the First World War.

Almost a hundred years have passed since Father Eugene's visit: more than sixty years—just over my own life span—since Hanna's visit. It seems strange, and worse than strange to some, against that background, that I should come here to speak in commemoration of a British Ambassador killed by Irish Republicans.

It would not have seemed so strange to Hanna's companion on that tragic journey, her son, then eight years old, Owen Sheehy-Skeffington, who lived to combat what he called 'the crazy militarism' of the IRA—a fury which had yet to reach its ghastly crescendo when Owen died in the summer of 1970.

Eugene and Hanna, in their generations, had good and adequate reasons for coming here to speak as they did, and I believe that my reasons in our own time for speaking as I have done are also good and adequate. The murdered Ambassador was no enemy to Ireland, but a friend, nor did he represent a power hostile to Ireland.

His widow and his orphaned children have shown themselves friends of Ireland in a far deeper sense than many of those who arrogate that title to themselves. The dark and atavistic forces that caused the death of Christopher Ewart-Biggs are still at work and it is right for Irish people who seek to combat that baneful influence to continue to reflect on the significance of that event. Contemporary Britain is not to blame for the troubles of contemporary Ireland, North or South, nor can she solve those troubles, nor can pressure on her to solve them do anything but make them worse. American aid, which in the past transformed the social and political landscape of Ireland, should not be invoked to solve a problem which it cannot solve : a problem of relations between two historic communities in Ireland itself, deriving from a movement of population contemporaneous with European settlement in North America. There are those who seek the solution of the problem in the enforced emigration of the contemporary descendants of the seventeenth-century settlers. Americans of European descent may well discern certain flaws in such a solution. Americans of Irish descent might reflect that they are not as long established in this country as is, in Ireland, that community which has sometimes been called alien : the community of Ulster Protestants.

I am not appealing to you, as Americans, to come to Ireland's rescue, and therefore, I can have no rousing peroration. I know, however, that many Americans today are—wisely, as I think—extremely cautious about appeals for intervention in other countries. Such caution, applicable to governmental intervention should apply even more to non-governmental intervention : in this case, the raising of funds for a so-called 'war' which the people of Ireland do not want and most of whose victims are Irish.

To discourage, in every possible way, all such efforts here is important in the interests of Ireland. It may be even more important for the future that the younger generation of Americans of Irish descent should reject the traditional assumption that friendship to Ireland is demonstrated by enmity to Britain. We have to deal here not with diverging interests any longer, but with converging ones. The better, for example, are the relations between the governments and peoples of Ireland and Great Britain, the better are the conditions for improved relations between the communities in Northern Ireland, the essential basis for peace and progress, in the interests alike of all the peoples of Great Britain and Ireland, and of the people of the United States.

# 4

## Britain, Northern Ireland and the Republic: Attitudes, Options and a Positive Programme

*Delivered at University College, Oxford,*
*23 October 1979*

In this final lecture, I am concerned with attitudes to Northern Ireland, in both parts of Ireland and in Britain, with possible options permitted by those attitudes, and with the possibility of a positive programme. I am grateful to the Master, my friend Lord Goodman, and to the Fellows of University College, Oxford, for giving me this opportunity to give this concluding lecture in the most fitting place : in Christopher Ewart-Biggs's college.

In the first lecture in the series, in Dublin, I said that we were commemorating both a personality and an event. The personality as I said was that of a notably gifted and notably attractive human being. The event was a peculiarly ominous and symbolic one : the murder of an envoy. That event symbolized the continuing existence of a pathological element in the relations between two peoples.

That pathological element is still at work. During the present year, using similar methods to those used against Christopher Ewart-Biggs, it took the lives of, among others, Airey Neave and Lord Mountbatten. The murders of those two were also symbolic events. The

78

victims chosen, like Christopher Ewart-Biggs, were chosen as, in the grisly jargon of the murderers, 'prestige targets'. Airey Neave, had he lived, would probably have been Secretary of State for Northern Ireland in the present Government. Lord Mountbatten was chosen because he was a member of the Royal Family who spent his holidays in Ireland. All three were singled out for murder, as symbols of England, by Irishmen who hate England.

How many such Irishmen—or rather how many such Irish people—are there? It is important, I think, that leaders of public opinion in this country should be able to assess the answer to that question as accurately as possible in order to avoid, on the one hand, the extreme of the porcine generalization recently attributed to a Royal personage or, on the other hand, the extreme of the starry-eyed assumption that almost all Irish people totally reject the IRA. To answer this question accurately is essential for an accurate appreciation of the extent of the IRA threat and of the best methods of dealing with it. I propose therefore to go into a little detail on this point. We have some new data. Last week a respected body, the Economic and Social Research Institute of Dublin, published the results of a survey of attitudes in the Republic of Ireland relevant to the Northern Ireland problem. The item that made the headlines in most newspapers here was that just over 20 per cent of Irish people 'support the IRA'. The report did indeed show that 20.7 per cent support the IRA in some degree. It listed the degrees:

| | |
|---|---|
| Slightly supportive | 12.3% |
| Moderately supportive | 5.3% |
| Strongly supportive | 2.8% |

Politicians in the Republic profess themselves greatly surprised at that finding. I am not surprised by it and no one who has looked carefully—but carefully—at previous polls should be surprised either.

In the first of these lectures delivered in Dublin on 17 January 1978, I drew attention to the results of a poll then recently published by Father MacGréil. He put to his sample one question which helps to establish the size of the minority who do not like the English. He asked the question : 'Would you be happy if Britain were brought to her knees?' While 79.3 per cent of his sample disagreed with that, 17.1 per cent agreed. It is here that we are in the presence of what I have described as the pathological element in British-Irish relations. Commenting on that element and its influences, I said in Dublin :

It was an Irish vision of England that killed Christopher Ewart-Biggs. He died not because of what he was, but because of how the country which he represented could be seen in the country in which he represented it. . . . And that vision is by no means confined to the fanatical conspirators who were the instruments of the deed. The conspirators are possessed by that vision in an intense form. Many of the rest of us are pervaded by a nebulous form of it.

The possessed draw their strength from the pervaded.

The possessed derive, from the intensity of the vision which grips them, an abundant sense of justification. . . .

The pervaded flinch from the horrors perpetrated, but feed the sense of justification that makes it possible to go on perpetrating them.

As regards the size of that pathological element, having

in mind not only the 'happy at Britain's being brought to her knees' brigade, but answers to other pertinent questions in the MacGréil survey, I said: 'I would put genuine Anglophobes—the possessed and the heavily pervaded together—at around 20 per cent of the population.' You will understand therefore why I am not in any way surprised by the Economic and Social Research Institute's finding that 20.7 per cent of the population support the IRA in some degree. That is how it is, and this is a very considerable part of our common problem. I underestimated that myself before the publication of the MacGréil findings but there is no excuse for anyone going on underestimating it.

The ESRI survey also showed that 68 per cent of the population of the Republic want a united Ireland, and that 78 per cent—a significantly and oddly higher figure—want Britain to leave Northern Ireland.

Turning to Northern Ireland itself, the survey shows a very different picture. Only 16 per cent of the population of Northern Ireland want a united Ireland. Of that population, 72 per cent want to stay in the United Kingdom. Not only do 87 per cent of Northern Ireland Protestants want that, but 49 per cent of Northern Ireland Catholics also want it. Only 39 per cent of Catholics in Northern Ireland, with 6 per cent of Protestants, want any kind of united Ireland.

Considering the figures for the Republic and for Northern Ireland together, the compilers of the survey ask this question, about the attitude of the people of *the whole island of Ireland*: 'Is there majority support for a united Ireland?' And the answer: 'Certainly not a clear majority.' They put support for a united Ireland at somewhere between 48 and 52 per cent of the whole population of Ireland.

This is important, because the traditional case for a united Ireland rests on the *assertion* that the whole island is the natural unit of democratic determination, and on the *assumption* that there is an overwhelming majority for unity among the population of the whole island. Speaking here at Oxford, to the British-Irish Association, two years ago, I cast doubt on that assumption and was vigorously, though vaguely, denounced for so doing. It is now clear that the assumption of overwhelming support for unity is quite untenable and that the population of the island of Ireland is about evenly divided as to whether the island should be united or not.

Does that degree of support for unity among the whole population of the island warrant the application of pressure against the great majority of the people of Northern Ireland who don't want to be incorporated in a united Ireland? I don't think that it does. The case becomes weaker still when we consider a further revelation of attitudes contained in the ESRI survey: attitudes of people in the Republic towards Northern Ireland Protestants. Those who like these Protestants—in *any* degree —add up to just 7.1 per cent. That is made up of:

| | |
|---|---|
| Strongly pro | 0.1% |
| Moderately pro | 0.7% |
| Slightly pro | 6.3% |

That is the extent of the affection which exists among the people of the Republic towards the people with whom, in theory, they yearn to be united.

Those in the Republic who actively *dis*like Northern Ireland Protestants outnumber those who like them at all by more then ten to one. The antis number 74.4 per cent, made up as follows:

| | |
|---|---|
| Slightly anti | 27.6% |
| Moderately anti | 29.1% |
| Strongly anti | 17.7% |

Comparing these findings with those of the MacGréil survey about attitudes of Dubliners to English people, we find that those in the Republic who dislike Northern Ireland Protestants appear to be about four times as numerous as those who dislike the English, while those who like the English are more than *ten* times as numerous as those who like Northern Ireland Protestants.

It may seem strange that this cluster of attitudes *towards people* should be combined with a political claim for 'Brits Out'. The Brits, whom most of us like, are to go, and the Prots, whom hardly any of us like, it seems, are to stay. . . . Or are they really?

In any case, it should not seem strange, in the light of these responses, that Northern Ireland Protestants should not be enthusiastic about being incorporated in a State, the majority of whose inhabitants would entertain such dispositions towards them—despite the professions of goodwill which they hear so often from the lips of politicians in the Republic.

Before I conclude the 'attitudinal' part of my discourse, and come to the limited range of options which the attitudes examined may permit, let me refer to what a recent survey (RTE and Gallup) has to say about attitudes in Britain towards options on Northern Ireland. That survey shows no majority in favour of any option. Only 25 per cent favour Northern Ireland's remaining part of the United Kingdom. Low though that degree of preference is, it is still higher than that in favour of any single option. In Britain, 21 per cent want a united Ireland; 24 per cent want an independent Northern Ireland —something wanted at present by hardly anyone in Ireland, North or South; 13 per cent want joint control by Britain and the Republic, and 17 per cent don't know —or admit that they don't know.

Let us now consider the implications which the attitudes surveyed, in both parts of Ireland and in Britain, have for the future.

Anyone who carefully considers these attitudes, and their distribution, has to realize, I think, that, where Northern Ireland is concerned, we are in for a prolonged period of instability and uncertainty, associated with at least a significant degree of violence, and involving serious danger of further deterioration, leading to violence on a far greater scale than anything yet experienced.

The cause of political violence in Ireland today is pressure meeting with resistance : pressure of most Irish Catholics towards unification of the island, meeting with the resistance of almost all Ulster Protestants to being incorporated in a united Ireland.

The recent survey, like previous surveys, suggests that both the pressure and the resistance are likely to continue. Most people in the Republic continue to call for unity, and a significant minority of them—those who give some degree of support to the IRA—are prepared to condone violence directed towards that end. This combination is probably enough to keep the political pressure, and the violent pressure, going on for quite a long time. These forms of pressure complement and encourage one another. Those who exert the political pressure take care to condemn the violence, but at the same time make political use of the existence of violence as their main argument. They call for 'fresh initiatives' designed to end the violence, and by fresh initiatives, they invariably mean shoving the Protestants to get them to move—just a little bit will do for a start—in the direction in which they refuse to go. And those who apply the violent pressure can claim, very convincingly, that they are the cutting edge of the policy demands insisted on by those who apply the political pressure.

So the pressure goes on. And, as every election and every survey shows, the resistance goes on too. The core of that resistance is constituted by the Protestants of Northern Ireland. But as the ESRI survey shows, half the Catholics of Northern Ireland also are not looking for unity. The pro-unity people, who are 68 per cent in the Republic, are only 39 per cent of Catholics in Northern Ireland. The reason for this differential is, I believe, that Northern Catholics have a much clearer and more personal idea of where pressure towards unity can lead, and of what would follow British withdrawal, than people yet have in the Republic.

Those who are carrying on the present campaign of violence know well that they cannot convince a majority in Northern Ireland. Their reasoning is : 'Brits Out, then we will deal with the Prots.' The second part of this is a colossal overestimation of their own capability. But the idea that the first objective—Brits Out—is attainable, is encouraged by the results of every survey of opinion in Britain, all of which show that most people in Britain would like to be rid of Northern Ireland.

The state of British public opinion, the state of public opinion in the Republic, the state of Irish-American public opinion (on which I have spoken elsewhere), all provide encouragement for the IRA to keep on killing. They also encourage Protestant paramilitaries to kill, and prepare themselves for a possible 'final solution'.

I have scanned this forbidding landscape of attitudes, not in order to make people's flesh creep, but because it is a landscape in which the problem is situated, and because wishful thinking about it is making things that are inherently dangerous more dangerous still.

I have stressed in this series of lectures, and in many other statements, the negative and intractable aspects of this situation, because I think that to minimize these aspects is a recipe for disaster, and because I feel that that disaster may not be far off—perhaps not more than ten years away.

However, it is fitting that in this, the concluding lecture in this commemorative series, I should spell out, not only what *should not* be done and said, but also—in more detail than I have done before—what *should* be said and done, by the British Government, by the Government in the Republic, and by people inside and outside Ireland and Britain who want to see Ireland progress towards peace, through improving relations between the different sections of its people.

What can Britain do towards this end?

First, British leaders should make a greater effort to explain to their own people why Britain is in Northern Ireland—or, more exactly, why Northern Ireland is in the United Kingdom and also what the basis of British policy in relation to this matter is. Northern Ireland is in the United Kingdom because the great majority of its people so desire. I think there are a great many people in Britain who do not know that. They should also tell them that it is British policy to allow Northern Ireland to remain in the United Kingdom as long as the majority of the people there want that; and also British policy to allow them to join a united Ireland when they show, by majority vote, that they so wish. These are reasonable policies and I believe that if they had ever been properly explained to the British people, there would be a great deal more support for having Northern Ireland in the United Kingdom than that miserable 25 per cent of today. To raise and maintain the level of support for that in Britain would probably do more than any other single thing to convince the IRA that they are not winning. Broadcast statements by the leaders of the three parties in Britain could be very helpful here. And these would also attract international attention, having a benign effect. They should spell out, not only the reasons for remaining in Northern Ireland, but the dire consequences which would follow withdrawal: civil war in Ireland, from the results of which, Britain, next door, could not be immune.

Second, inside Northern Ireland, the British Government should—as indeed they are doing—try to set up such representative institutions as can be set up without frightening or incensing members of either community. Here a double veto comes into play. The Catholics in effect veto democratic institutions of normal type, because they fear these mean restored Protestant rule. The Protestant leaders veto special 'power sharing' or 'participatory' institutions, because they suspect these are intended as the start on a slippery slope towards unification —and the fact that the Republic and the SDLP are demanding that pressure be put on Protestants to accept power sharing does nothing to diminish that suspicion. Under these conditions, it appears that the only type of institution which would have a chance of acceptance in both communities would be one without executive or legislative power: in effect, a Consultative Assembly, in which members could question the Secretary of State, offer their advice to him, debate the workings of the various Departments of State, and have access to these, on behalf of their constituents. This would not be a substitute for direct rule, but it would do much to fill the famous 'vacuum' of democracy which exists under direct rule, and it would thereby improve the working of direct rule.

It is necessary to stress once more that surveys have shown that direct rule is the only form of government which has been found acceptable by a majority in both communities. Those who want to de-stabilize direct rule therefore are seeking to replace something acceptable in *both* communities by something acceptable in one community only—a good recipe for increased disorder and violence. I therefore hope that the Secretary of State, when his consultations are completed, will be able to institute some kind of Consultative Assembly, helping him to make direct rule more sensitive to legitimate demands of the Northern Ireland public.

I do not think that Britain can do much more than that, by way of political initiative, without causing more harm than good. What can the government of the Republic do?

No one who studies the attitudinal profile of the population of the Republic, as it defines itself in the ESRI survey and other surveys, can avoid having some sympathy with the leader of the governing party, as he handles this delicate problem. He must be careful always, about that dangerous 20 per cent—which he prefers, understandably—to think of as 2 per cent. He knows that there are many more than that, even in his own party. None the less, he is assured—as the survey also shows—of majority support in taking more stringent measures against the IRA and in closer co-operation with the security forces in Northern Ireland. A survey carried out in the Republic by RTE in the wake of the Mountbatten and Warrenpoint murders showed 80 per cent in favour of direct signalling communication between the Irish and British Armies on the border in the pursuit and apprehension of terrorists. The governing party is clearly free to move in the direction of closer security co-operation, and I believe it is moving in that direction.

What more can the leader of the governing party do, that would help, without hurting himself politically, which should not be expected of him? I can think of one thing more that he can do and one thing less.

The 'one thing less' is to desist in future from suggesting or implying that there is some fresh political initiative which it is in the power of the British Government to take, which would have the effect of ending the violence. He should not suggest that, because it is not true, and because continued pressure on Britain to do the impossible makes it more likely that Britain will eventually withdraw from Northern Ireland, thus plunging all Ireland into civil war.

That brings me to the 'one thing *more*' that the governing party can do. That is to explain to the people of the Republic the damage that precipitate British withdrawal —there are reasons why he would have to say 'precipitate'—could bring to *the people of the Republic*. I emphasize those last five words for reasons which I shall now make clear.

89

## Britain, Northern Ireland and the Republic

The survey from which I have quoted so much contains one curious feature which has puzzled commentators. A majority of respondents—57 per cent—showed themselves aware that British withdrawal would result in a great increase in violence : 37 per cent think that that would be the only consequence; 20.5 per cent think there would be violence and a settlement. None the less, 71 per cent still want the British to withdraw. Even some of those who think that the only result of withdrawal would be increased violence think that.

How come? Is it that all these people are so ardent for British withdrawal that they think any of the risks to their own lives, to their children, to their property, are worthwhile? I do not believe this, and other data suggest that this is not the case. For example, only a minority of the sample declared any willingness to pay higher taxes for a united Ireland. Civil war is a great deal nastier than higher taxes, though it also requires those. I am afraid that the reason for this enthusiasm for a course which is seen by a majority as resulting in 'greater violence' is that respondents think of the violence, and other nasty consequences, as occurring only in Northern Ireland. The violence, they imagine, would be happening to other people. The leader of the governing party, who well understands the dangers, should disillusion his people. The consequences for the Republic would be shattering too. When I was in the Government of the Republic, in 1975, I asked two leading members of the SDLP what would be the dimensions of the influx of refugees which we in the Republic would have to expect, in the event of British withdrawal from Nothern Ireland being followed by great violence. They conferred briefly and came back with the answer : 55,000 to 65,000 *families*—approximately 250,000 people—half the Catholic population of Northern Ireland. An influx on that scale, without considering other dire and inevitable consequences, would ruin the Republic—socially, institutionally and economically. If the leader of the governing party would get that message over to his fellow citizens, he would sensibly lessen their enthusiasm for British withdrawal, and diminish the pressures on himself in that direction.

The steps I have suggested would have the effect of making conditions throughout these islands significantly less propitious for terrorists, and more propitious towards progress to peace.

But something more is called for. The necessarily quite modest political initiatives are useful, but they are not enough. Something much larger is needed; something large and constructive; something that could warm people's imaginations; something that would bring at least some hope to Northern Ireland, and ring around the world with a message of creative and neighbourly endeavour.

Is something of that order possible? I think so, and I think I discern its outlines, though at some distance still.

I do not think such an initiative is available in the *political* domain. The pattern of attitudes which I have surveyed at perhaps tedious length should be enough to establish that. Any major new political initiative—above the modest level of consultative institutions—is certain to be bitterly divisive, and the main new initiative which is possible—British withdrawal—would be not merely divisive but catastrophic.

Those who call for fresh political initiatives are barking up the wrong tree. They are not wrong to look for fresh initiatives: they should just delete the word 'political'. The fresh initiatives that would be constructive and not divisive are to be found, I believe, in the economic and social spheres. What I have in mind is the application, in conditions adapted to Northern Ireland, of the principles of the Marshall and Monnet Plans.

It would be similar to the Marshall Plan, in that it would be a funding effort of reconstruction, coming from abroad and leaving the allocation of the funds in local hands.

It would be based on the same thinking as Jean Monnet applied to Europe : seeking to transcend ancient rancours, or by-pass them, through a common economic effort. But there would also be differences, necessitated by the grim realities of Northern Ireland. The OECD and EEC—sprung, the one from the initiative of George Marshall, the other from that of Jean Monnet—are basically inter-governmental organizations, led at national level by politicians. Nothing directly like that could succeed in Northern Ireland. Granted the constitutional controversy over Northern Ireland, and the bitterly and chronically divisive nature of politics inside Northern Ireland, any effort to work through governmental and political channels would be doomed to failure. You will remember how President Carter made an offer of American economic aid to Northern Ireland, *conditional* upon progress towards a political settlement. That offer perished, strangled in its own political strings. So it would be with any attempt to work a scheme of this kind through governmental or political channels. What is needed is aid without strings, aid for the sake of actually helping people, not just for an ulterior political move.

Let me be a little more precise—although I cannot yet be very precise—about what I have in mind. It is the

institution, first, of a Northern Ireland Fund, internation-
ally and privately financed, and then of a Northern Ireland Development Corporation, composed of private
citizens, interested in the allocation of those funds for
the benefit of the people of Northern Ireland. Such a
development would require the assent of the British
Government—which I cannot think would be withheld
—and it could benefit from an intimation of the approval
of the Irish Government. More is not required of either
Government, at least until the scheme should come into
full operation when of course it would require co-
operation from government departments in Northern
Ireland.

In establishing the Northern Ireland Fund, what
would be needed is the interest, first, of philanthropic
foundations, and then of industry and of the international
trade-union movement. The first step to be taken is discussion of the matter in an appropriate non-governmental international forum; the second is the carrying
out of a feasibility study, again under private international auspices. I am confident that the first two steps
can and will be taken. The next steps depend on the outcome of the feasibility study. If that outcome is positive
—as I think it will be—then I am confident that the support of foundations, industry, the trade-union movement
and private citizens can be enlisted, and that a fund can
be generated on a scale sufficient to make a very considerable impact on Northern Ireland's social and economic problems, and having—in conjunction with the
other step here suggested—benign long-term effects on
its political problems also.

The Northern Ireland Development Corporation will
come into being only if the Fund comes into being. The

Corporation should be composed of private citizens of Northern Ireland, mainly drawn from industry, finance and the trade-union movement. The reason for such a composition is that industrialists, financiers, and trade unionists are constantly conscious of having something to lose—business and jobs—and so are strongly motivated in the direction of development and peace and not in the direction of confrontation and point-scoring. The record of the Northern Ireland trade unions in keeping sectarian violence out of places of work is also relevant. There should be no politicians, not because politicians are necessarily bad, but because of the antagonistic nature of Northern Ireland politics. There are two people who I hope would serve on it, because of their personalities and of what they symbolize, both to Ireland and throughout the world: the Peace Women, Betty Williams and Máiread Corrigan.

The central problem which such a Corporation would have to tackle is obvious: the economically stagnant, high-unemployment areas of Northern Ireland. That problem should be tackled for its own sake, but its solution would also have wider social and political effects. It would tend to diminish sectarian resentments. It would deprive the men of violence of their most fertile recruiting grounds, and of the social and economic elements in the bitterness on which they feed. Above all, it would bring hope, some light at the end of the long dark tunnel that these last ten years have been.

A pipe dream? Maybe. There seems, at any rate, enough substance in it, prima facie, to warrant further study. It may be said that these are very large and ambitious plans to be put forward by a private citizen, with no representative capacity. But it is precisely because I am a private citizen, and unrepresentative, that I am able to put it forward here in the form I have explained. No politician would care much for something with no role for politicians and anything with such a role would be doomed by the terrible political–sectarian divisions which constitute the problem. The politicians have been doing little in this area, except calling on other politicians to do things which they know in advance they are not going to do. The initiative I propose is at any rate a little more promising than that kind of activity.

I have put forward these ideas—both here and more quietly elsewhere—and will pursue them, as a private citizen with some international contacts and communications.

I am putting them forward practically in the context of this lecture, because the best way to commemorate Christopher Ewart-Biggs, and all the others who have died because of this dispute that torments both our islands, is to try to find a rational course of action that will tend to diminish, rather than enlarge, the scale of future deaths from political violence.

I cited at the outset the names of Airey Neave and Lord Mountbatten, together with that of Christopher Ewart-Biggs. I cited them because they belong with him in one particular, symbolic category of victims. But I know that they would wish us here to commemorate along with them also all the thousands of victims of political violence arising from this dispute in and over Ireland : Irish and British people, Protestants, Catholics, agnostics, men, women and children. I think of the living victims as well as the dead, the wounded, the maimed, the incapacitated, the widowed, the orphaned, and among these that most poignant category of all—the children now growing up who have seen a parent murdered before their eyes.

We commemorate the dead best by trying to help the living and we help the living best—in dealing with the dangerous effects of a complex political dispute—when we use our minds properly: not allowing our thinking to be dominated by inherited prejudice and unexamined assumptions or to be distorted by the desire to believe what we wish were true, when the evidence suggests that it is not. What is needful is that reason should apply itself to the purposes of compassion, and that compassion should accept the guidance of reason towards the fulfilment of those purposes.